Success Is A Choice
Unveiling the truth

Table of Contents

Success Is A Choice

Unveiling the truth

Obakeng Mosime

Success Is A Choice
Unveiling the truth

Obakeng Mosime is an Entrepreneur, Author, Investor, and a Financial Market Analyst. Born and bred in Kuruman - Northern Cape (South Africa). He dedicatedly solves people's problems through the services he offers. He defines it as the purpose of his life and what truly brings him meaning.

Dedication

To my dearest Son Lonwabo Obakeng Jr. "Ljay"
This book is dedicated to you with all my love, admiration, and pride. You have been my greatest source of aspiration and motivation in everything I do and your mother's unwavering support and encouragement have been the fuel that has propelled me towards my dreams. As I wrote this book, I couldn't help but think of you and the amazing person you will become.
Your mother's determination, passion, and resilience have taught me that success is indeed a choice. Her unwavering faith and abilities have shown me that anything is possible if we put our minds to it.
I hope this book inspires you to pursue your dreams and never give up on your goals. May it serve as a reminder that success is not something that happens to us, but rather, it is something we choose.
Thank you for being my son and my constant source of joy.
I am so proud of you and I love you more than words can express.
With all my love
Obakeng Mosime

Contents

Introduction

In this book we will explore the idea that success is a choice. We will delve into the power of the mind and the impact it has on our ability to achieve success in all areas of life. We will also examine the societal and cultural factors that can influence our beliefs about success and how to overcome them. This book will also provide you with practical solutions and step by step guide to escape poverty. As the world spins in chaos and confusion, many of us are left wondering what the true meaning of success is. We are told that success is measured by wealth, power, and fame, but is this really the case? Or is there something deeper, something more profound, that lies at the heart of success? The truth is, success is a choice. It is a choice to break free from the illusions and lies that have been fed to us by the controlling elite. It is a choice to awaken to our true potential and live a life of purpose and fulfillment.

For too long we have been manipulated and controlled by those in power. We have been led to believe that success is something that is handed to us. Rather than something we must actively pursue.

We have been taught to chase after external markets of success, rather than focusing on our own personal growth and development. But the truth is, true success is not about accumulating wealth or attaining fame. It is about becoming the best version of ourselves, and living a life of meaning and purpose. It is about breaking free from the shackles of control and manipulation, and embracing our true potential. To truly be successful, we must make the choice to awaken to the truth. We must choose to break free from the illusions that have been fed to us, and to see the world for what it truly is. We must choose to take control of our own lives and live them to the fullest. This is not an easy path to take, but it is the only path that leads to true success. It requires hard work , perseverance, and a willingness to constantly strive for personal growth. But if we make the choice to pursue success, we have the power to achieve our greatest aspirations and to live a life of freedom and fulfillment. So, as you navigate the complexities of this world, remember that success is a choice, the choice is yours.

Chapter 1

CAPITAL CHRONICLES: The myth of scarcity

Hailing from the scorching, sun-drenched terrain of Northern Cape, specifically the revered locality of Kuruman, a small town that has shaped my identity and influenced my journey towards success. A place where vastness of the landscape meets the boundless spirit of it's people. Nested amidst breathtaking natural beauty, Kuruman is a town that resonates with a deep sense of tranquility. As I reflect on my upbringing in Kuruman, I am reminded of the values instilled in me. It is here that I learned the significance of perseverance in the face of adversity.

The rich history of Kuruman, dating back to prehistoric times, adds depth to my understanding of the place I call home. From the indigenous San people who roamed these lands, leaving behind remnants of their ancient wisdom, to the missionaries who brought education and enlightenment, each chapter of Kuruman's past has contributed to the vibrant mosaic that shapes my present. I am blessed with natural wonders that ignite my imagination and fuel my determination.

The majestic Eye of Kuruman, a crystal – clear spring that has quenched the thirst of generations, symbolizes the eternal wellspring of opportunity and possibility that exists within my reach. It serves as a reminder that success is not confined to external circumstances but is nurtured from within, drawing from the deep well of our own potential.

I have honed an unwavering attentiveness to my surroundings. Through this observance, I have arrived at the stark realization that a vast majority of individuals are perpetually trapped within an unyielding cycle of impoverishment, tragically oblivious to their own plight.

The human spirit no longer appears to harbor the same unyielding tenacity for the realization of its aspirations. This fact is one that I have borne witness to firsthand, born from my upbringing and experiences. Recently, a conversation with a fellow individual crystallized this unfortunate reality. He resigned himself from the notion that is nigh impossible to ascend to the echelons of multi-millionaire status, particularly when hailing from the humble environs of Kuruman. His sole ambition was to procure a job at the local mine, acquire a vehicle through debt, and subsist paycheck to paycheck, blithely disregarding the fragility of his position. For what if calamity befalls him and he finds himself unceremoniously out of employment? What if he were to become a victim of workplace downsizing or redundancy? The imperative here is clear, one must always have a comprehensive, well-plotted strategy in place, not one that leads to further impoverishment, but rather one that will lift them from their current state of destitution and propel them towards the lofty height of success.

A disheartening reality has set in among our fellow human beings, a surrender of sorts to the notion that their aspirations are unattainable. The self-deprecating attitude that pervades our society has relegated the pursuit of success to a select few. I am witness to my contemporaries, individuals with whom I shared a scholastic journey, opting to settle for mediocrity. That is not to imply that I myself have surmounted the pinnacle of achievement or accrued vast riches. I am, however, committed to my quest to scale the heights of success, and this book is an earnest attempt to impart a blueprint of how one may do the same. It is disconcerting to witness the pervasive culture of grievance and excuse-making that envelops our society, leading individuals down the perilous path of insurmountable debt and a hand-to-mouth existence.

As we progress through life, our desires and aspirations undergo a natural evolution, rendering our previous wants and needs as outdated and irrelevant. Such is my personal experience, as the superfluous trappings of youth that preoccupied my mind at the age 22 have been replaced by a laser-like focus on investment opportunities, land acquisition, and infrastructure development. The pursuit of such endeavors is the hallmark of a purposeful existence. The time has come to re-calibrate our priorities, to relinquish and embrace a more consequential path in life. Those born in the 90s ought to be attuned to the pressing economic issues at hand, toiling relentlessly to ensure they approach their 30s with a secure financial footing. This is why I toil unceasingly, endeavoring to build an enviable legacy for my progeny, my beloved son, Lonwabo.

The more I learn about money and risk management, the more I realize that people don't truly have an affection for money, but rather a strong desire for it. When you love something, you cherish and take care of it, nurturing it as it grows. However, when you have a lust for something, you use it to your advantage and discard it. This is similar to the way people treat money.

They acquire it quickly but often lose it just as fast. If individuals genuinely loved money, they would save and invest it to help it grow, rather than squandering it. In modern times, relationships are similar in that people often lust after one another rather than love and work to grow together.

Our problem is laziness and caring too much about the opinions of others while we have nothing. Let's hustle, let's do whatever it takes for the dream. Our brothers from neighboring countries come to South Africa not having much yet within 3 to 5 years, they have strong and lucrative businesses.

This should tell you that there's plenty of money in South Africa, regardless of the current state of economy. Do not believe if someone tells you that there's no money. Find a way to take that money and put it in your pockets and create a business, and out of that money hire the same people. Making plus R500 a day is still possible through just hustling. All you need is just an idea and correct use of information.

After getting the money, make sure you return it back by buying land. Not just land, but a farm. People who farm or own such land, control us. People with food, control us. They can starve us if they decide not to farm anymore and money will be useless hence why we are nothing without farmers. If we can experience lack of electricity, it shows lack of food security is next in few years time. So grow your own food, tough times are coming.

The problem is you're no longer hungry for your dreams. You've gotten used to your comfort zone and this is why, everything you are trying to do doesn't work out, because nothing challenges you anymore. When you do this and that, you easily give up because you're home.

Try to hustle a 5 thousand rands for a 2 month rent. Pack your bags, move out from your comfort zone and go to a different location where you're unknown. Then see if that location won't force you to work hard and get the best out of you. When you get to that place, forget about girls and vices. Be a ghost. What do I mean by being a ghost? Disappear from the limelight of doing things to please people. Be there to make money and nothing else. Being and staying alone makes you think and focus more. You will see when you get there, you will have new ideas and you will act upon them because your rent is first priority. That's going to make you strive harder and look for opportunities.

You're relaxed and not applying any pressure towards your dreams because you're home, where you get everything handed to you on a silver platter. Success is about taking risks. We all have the same 24hours, it is completely up to you how you use yours.

In today's world, many of us are conditioned to believe that money is a scarce resource. We are taught that we must work hard, save diligently, and sacrifice our time and energy in order to accumulate enough money to live a comfortable life.

But what if I told you that this scarcity mindset is a myth? What if I told you that money is not a finite resource, but rather an endless stream of abundance that is available to all of us? The truth is, money is not a scarce resource. It is not something that must be earned through hard work and sacrifice. Instead, it is a fluid and ever-changing system of exchange that is constantly flowing through our lives.

To understand the true nature of money, we must first recognize that it is not a tangible object. It is not a physical thing that can be held, touched, or stored. Instead, it is a symbol of value that represents the exchange of goods and services. In other words, money is simply a means of exchange. It is a tool that we use to facilitate transactions and trade. And because it is not a physical thing, there is no limit to how much of it can be created or exchanged.

The idea of scarcity is simply a myth that has been perpetuated by those who seek to control the flow of money. They want us to believe that there is a limited supply of money, so that we will work harder and consume less, allowing them to maintain their power and control over the system. But the truth is, money is not controlled by any one person or group. It is a system that is open to all of us, and we all have the power to participate in it and benefit from it. So how do we tap into this endless stream of abundance? How do we move beyond the scarcity mindset and unlock the power of money in our lives?

The first step is to recognize that our beliefs about money are not based in reality. We must acknowledge that we have been conditioned to believe that money is scarce, and that this belief is not serving us. The second step is to shift our mindset from scarcity to abundance. We must begin to see money as a fluid and ever-changing system of exchange that is available to all of us, rather than a limited resource that must be hoarded and protected. The third step is to take action. We must actively seek out opportunities to create value and contribute to the world around us. We must be willing to take risks, to try new things, and to push ourselves beyond our comfort zones. And finally, we must be willing to share our abundance with others. When we give freely and generously, we create a positive energy that attracts even more abundance into our lives.

Money is one of the most powerful tools we have in our modern society. It has the ability to transform lives, create opportunities, and even change the world. And yet, we have been taught to believe that money is scarce, and that only a lucky few can truly achieve financial success. This is a lie. The truth is that money is endless. It is not a finite resource that we must struggle to earn and fight to keep. It is a fluid and ever-changing system of exchange that is available to all of us. We have been brainwashed to believe in the scarcity mindset because those in power want to maintain their control over us.

The myth of scarcity has been ingrained in us since childhood. We have been taught that money is hard to come by, that we must work hard and sacrifice our time and energy to accumulate enough of it to survive. But the reality is that money is not a physical thing. It is a tool that we use to facilitate transactions and trade.

The scarcity mindset has been used to keep us obedient and submissive. Those in power want us to believe that the only way to get ahead is to follow their path to success, which often involves working harder and longer, sacrificing our time and energy, and accepting their authority over us. But we don't have to accept this lie.

We have the power to shift our mindset from scarcity to abundance. We can recognize that the myth of scarcity is a lie perpetuated by those who seek to control us. We can take control of our own lives and create our own opportunities.

The first step in shifting our mindset is to recognize the power of money. Money is not just a tool for survival. It is a tool for growth and transformation. When we recognize the power of money to transform our lives, we can start to create abundance.

The next step is to take action. We must be willing to take risks and try new things. We must push ourselves beyond our comfort zones and challenge the status quo. We must stand up to those who seek to control us and demand our fair share of the abundance that is available to us. One way to take action is to start a business or invest in yourself. Entrepreneurship is one of the most powerful ways to create abundance. By starting your own business, you have the potential to create unlimited wealth and achieve financial freedom.

Investing in yourself is another powerful way to create abundance. By investing in your education, skills, and personal development, you can increase your earning potential and unlock new opportunities for yourself. But it's not just about taking action for yourself. It's also about giving back to others. When we give freely and generously, we create a positive energy that attracts even more abundance into our lives. Generosity can take many forms. It can be as simple as volunteering your time or donating to charity. It can also be as complex as creating a business that provides value to society and creates jobs.

When we give freely and generously, we create a ripple effect that can change the world. The more we give, the more we receive. And the more abundance we create, the more we can share with others. It's time to break free from the myth of scarcity and embrace the power of abundance. We must recognize that money is endless and that we have the power to create our own success. We must be willing to take action, to push ourselves beyond our comfort zones, and to give freely and generously to others. As I reflect on the state of our continent, I am struck by the pervasive belief that children must suffer just as their parents did. Such defeatist mindset surrenders to the grasp of weakness. And undermines the fundamental purpose of parenthood.

We must aspire for our offspring to surpass us, to have access to opportunities that we never did, to be nourished and clothed appropriately, and to attend the finest educational institutions. Our responsibility as parents is to endow the next generation with the resources to embark upon life's journey. The root of Africa's enduring poverty lies in the notion that children must have nothing. This mindset emanates from the minds of defeated people. In start contrast, the white community grasps the notion that their offspring must have everything.

It is a lesson that is ingrained from one generation to the next, resulting in the accumulation of wealth that endures through time. Wealth that is passed down from father to son, assuring that even those who are yet to be born are already provided for. They have learned that suffering is an unnecessary affliction, and should be prevented whenever possible. Tragically, here in Africa, we have become enamored with the idea that poverty is a virtue, an expression of our culture.

We have embraced the notion that our children must inherit the misery that we have endured. We have even hidden our wealth in death, depriving our heirs of the resources that we ourselves have accumulated. In doing so, we are moving backward, not forward, undermining the very essence of progress. We must embrace embrace the opposite of suffering endowing our children with everything, so that they may prosper, and in turn provide their own offspring, ensuring that our legacy endures for generations to come.

" We must recognize that money is endless and that we have the power to create our own success."
- Obakeng Mosime

" We must recognize that money is endless and that we have the power to create our own success."
- Obakeng Mosime

Chapter 2

SUCCESS OR SETBACK : The power of your choices

As I reflect upon the challenges faced by individuals within my country, I have arrived at a conclusion that the decisions we make have the potential to either propel us towards a fulfilling and prosperous life or result in a detrimental outcome. In light of living in a democratic society, it is evident that the landscape of our nation has undergone a transformation over the past few decades.

Success is no longer contingent upon one's race, whether they are white, black, or any other skin color. While some may argue that equal opportunities are not readily accessible, such a notion should not serve as an excuse for a lack of achievement. In fact, there are an abundance of opportunities available to individuals if they take the initiative to seek them out. Unfortunately, many individuals are inclined to shift the blame to external factors such as limited resources or government policies rather than taking responsibility for their own efforts.

I strongly believe that this perspective is merely an excuse and a reflection of a lack of motivation to put in the necessary work to attain success. To truly achieve one's goals, it is essential to take the initiative and create opportunities rather than passively waiting for success to fall into one's lap.

I am of the belief that every individual must come to a point in their lives where they must make a conscious decision to either strive for success or accept the potential for setbacks and possible failure due to a lack of effort. While it is natural to view setbacks as failures, it is important to recognize their significance in the learning process, as they serve as opportunities to learn valuable lessons and make corrections that facilitate progress towards success.

Ultimately, the key to success lies in one's mindset, specifically whether they possess a winning mentality or not. It can be difficult to make decisions, as the long-term outcomes of these choices are often unclear at the time of decision-making. As such, taking calculated risks is crucial to achieving success and ascending the ladder while building a prosperous empire. When it comes down to it, there are only two choices available: a positive one that moves us forward or a negative one that sets us back. There is no such thing as a neutral choice when it comes to achieving success.

Let us dabble a bit on everyone's favorite topic shall we...Money! If You look around it seems to be the number one thing everyone wants to acquire. So how does one get to have money? I was reading Forbes Magazine few months ago while sitting in my room reminiscing about life in general, And Half way through the book, I could already see a repetitive pattern of how the top 1% that made it to Billionaire status actually managed to make it through the hurdles on their path to success.

I have seen people get money fast and lose it all in just a few months, Because they were not ready for success . People want success but in the same breath they're not actually ready for success. Risk management plays a huge role in accumulating wealth through the power of compound effect. The problem is People want to be rich overnight, I've seen my fellow brothers and sisters making loans for ridiculous interest rates, only to take that money and blow it all at the Casino.

This ends up being a cycle of doing the same thing over and over again. It's like being stuck in loop. People end up being in debt because their scared of things that don't even matter, they have what I call in My home language 'Batho ba tlo reng' - syndrome, Meaning 'What will the people say'. Driven by Ego is never a good thing, Sometimes You are the reason for your own demise.

People struggle to make ends meets, but prefer to make debts just to paint this perfect image for people that don't even care about them. Hence the mind is a very powerful thing, we have the conscious mind and the sub-conscious mind. We use our sub-conscious mind to manifest things to life. Your mind has the power to influence your behavior.

That's why most of the times when you need to make a decision, you are in some sort of a predicament when you find yourself not knowing what choice to make. That's because your conscious mind and your sub-conscious are constantly in a conversation, your thoughts are split between what's wrong, what's right, positive and negative thoughts flow throughout day and night in your mind.

Learn how to control your mind and control your life. Filter out how you spend your time. Are you feeding your mind the right or wrong information? What kind of music do you listen to? What king of information do you get from YouTube videos. What articles or tweets are you feeding your mind? Reason for the questions is because thoughts play a major role in our life and determines whether we will achieve success or not. You have to program your mind to think in terms of Assets Over Liabilities. In simple terms an asset is something that generates income, a liability is something that takes money out its an expense. Money that comes in will get you closer to success, money that goes out will get you closer to poverty.

Learn to differentiate between the two before you make any decision when it comes to making a purchase. Ask yourself is this a Need or a Want? Can you afford it? Is it going to get you closer to success or poverty. In order to achieve success you must first fix your mindset and shift your perspective on how you view things. I don't know why black people like glorifying poverty.

They will get offended when you call black tax black tax. You're busy glorifying black tax while white people are creating generational wealth. Other races are creating wealth for the next generation and we are promoting the culture of taking care of our old generation and letting the new generation start from the bottom with nothing.

We need to stop glorifying poverty. Of course we paying black tax because our parents were oppressed. But our children must not take care of us. Imagine if our children have to take care of us and build from the bottom. That means our generations will always be poor. We thinking backwards. I don't expect a cent from my child. On top of that he will not start from nothing. He will have a business and wealth to inherit. I can't be telling my children black tax or Ubuntu is a culture nah. It ends with me. My children will not know what black tax is. All they will have to know is that they need to create wealth for the next generation.

Your friend is 25years old, he already has a house a car and getting married. While you on the other side nothing seems to be working out for you. Well you decide that you want to start a business. You actually want to compete with your friend. Your friend already owns a Sportscar. That affects you now because your coming into business with that mentality of I want to get rich overnight. It's your first year ever in business yet by December you want to be owning a brand new Sportscar.

That is when you start making stupid business decisions. Instead of you starting small and selling fat cookies or opening a chicken dust you want to go for that fancy business. By the time you reach age 30 you tell people that you've been hustling for 5 year's but you got nothing to show for it. Actually you haven't been hustling you've been competing and looking for short cuts. Your friend may buy a Sportscar at 25years but there's absolutely nothing wrong with your buying a Sportscar at 33 life is not a race. I know a guy whom at 31 had a degree struggled to find a job. He went and studied became a security guard. He worked for three year's as a security guard then opened his security company.

This year his turning 37 and his company makes R60000 pm he bought a house cash last year and this year his getting married. Some of his friends who were laughing at him when he was a security guard are still renting and don't qualify for bonds. My point is there's this kind of race going on in this generation, you see someone accomplishing something on social media then you also want to accomplish it overnight.

That squashes your creativity because now you have this urgency to make it overnight. I've learned the very hard way that there's nothing wrong with growing slow, competition is dangerous. No one is ahead or behind in life. Everyone has his own race. That's how you should look at it. From the ages of 5 we are told to worry about what people think about us. You go out to play and get dirty. When you come back your parents bear you up and ask you, " What will our neighbors say when they see you this dirty" You get pregnant or fail class " O re tsegisa ka makhelwane". This has now shaped the way we are living. I've seen people make seriously bad financial decisions because they were worried what other people will think of them.

I know a guy who bought a car he couldn't afford because he was worried what the neighbors will think if he bought a cheaper one. People are scared to go back to their parents houses even during tough economic times because they worried about the opinions of neighbors. This affects us for the rest of our lives. We should teach our children to worry only about their own opinions about themselves. Not what someone will think of them. Imagine there are people who can't take some jobs right now because they worried what people will think of them. They rather sleep with empty stomachs. It's difficult to shift the paradigm. When you die you go to the grave alone. At that time no one's opinion matters. Let's not pass this mentality to our children.

Let's teach them how to be mentally strong and shut down the outside noise. Never in my life have I seen a country like this. Where people are suffering from poverty but are hiding their struggle so well. That's South Africa for you. In other countries you can see poverty from afar people repeating clothes, waking up at 3am to sell stuff at the market etc. Here you will not see that. That's why people here have depression because they suffer from the inside.

This sense of humor we have makes it worse because we are laughing everyday on social media, yet in the inside we are crying for help. People have no job's here, those who have jobs are forced to take care of their families including nephews and nieces. Yes there are rich ones but only a few. The inequality is too much. The major problem is that here it's difficult to Identify the poor. A person with serious financial problems may wear clothes that are more expensive then the ones your wearing. Or a weave you will never afford or might be using an I Phone. Or posting pictures drinking expensive champagne. If you go from house to house and ask them what their struggle is. You will be shocked. People are struggling to pay rates in Townships and electricity. Some houses the electricity has been shut down. With a high teenage pregnancy rate house holds are being over crowded water,groceries and electricity is becoming too expensive. If you're one of the people suffering. Come out the closet before you find yourself having a depression.

I know it's difficult to come out because you think you're the only one but I'm telling you there's a lot of people suffering here. Go do whatever to make a living and to survive. Surviving has become harder and harder. South Africa is becoming one country with a beautiful infrastructure and poor citizens. The struggle is real I tell you, wake up do something even if you look like a fool it's fine long as you have something to eat. Stop trying so hard to hide your struggle by doing nothing you will die from depression.

We've got unemployed poor people wearing R5000 worth of hair also unemployed people drinking Hennessy. In the same family you find that there's only one person working and it a girl. She needs to take care of her mother whose earning pension money and the whole family including her sisters who wear R3000 worth of hair and her brother's who drink Hennessy on weekend's. Instead of them putting that money that they bought Hennessy and hair with together and starting a chicken dust business or something to support their families. We have many challenges that we are facing in our communities right now we choose to hide them with fake lifestyle.

How can one person take care of the whole family including adults who don't even want to support her yet they also ask her for money for clothes. Expensive clothes to wear in events so that they can look rich when they situation is on the ICU at home. Don't choose the fake lifestyle, be real. Support your family and toil. Don't be a burden to someone else. We need strong prayers for Instagram it's one major causes of suffering in our communities because people have become some kind of broke superstar's. Who are always in luxurious places. Girls would even go to a club buy one cocktail share it and take pictures with it. Just to pretend as if they are living the life. As things look right now a few are willing to face reality. I feel sorry for our elders who are the ones suffering the most from this fake life.

Owning a car gives your a certain amount of respect in the Township. You become a man of dignity. People don't even care whether you afford fuel and the service or not. Let's be honest buying a car puts you in another level. That's why when someone makes his first R100k or gets his first job he wants a car. He wants to be on that particular level. He wants respect from the society because no one take you serious when your still using taxis. Then again in reality owning a car doesn't mean your successful. Once you own a car you have many friends.

You visit too many people and you spend too much on fuel cost's. For some people a car is a necessity. I understand. But for some it's not much of a necessity it's just pressure from the society. That's one reason a lot of young people who bought cars or fancy cars by age 23 are broke today. They maintain the image but not the bank balance. Never allow society to put any amount of pressure on you. What society thinks will never put food on the table for you.

Stay in your own lane. "Don't fake it till you make it" Faking it might put you in serious debt especially in these days of trying to impress people on social media. There's a guy who went to Pretoria from Mozambique to study. When he got to Pretoria he identified I nice business opportunity. He saw a very busy area where he can put a mobile kitchen and sell food. But he needed R50000 capital he tried the banks and all his friends he still couldn't get the money.

He had a very rich uncle who never supported him. He decided that he was going to lie to his uncle in order to get the R50k. So Him and his other friend's who were studying medicine and training. Decided that they were going to fake an accident. They had all the material even the scans and pictures. They sent everything home. The guy told his family that his in a critical condition and needs R55000 for an operation. The uncle deposited the money instantly. The guy gave his doctor friends R5000 took R50000 got his mobile kitchen. He was not making less than R1000 a day in less than 3 month's he paid of his uncles debt and told his whole family the truth about what happened. They we're first angry at him but grateful because the guy was now able to send money home every month instead of his straggling mother sending him money. The moral of the story is. If you lack resources and there's a risk to be taken then take it. Stop complaining. Not every billionaire you see today was born with a silver spoon on his mouth most come from very poor backgrounds.

Some people are not getting anywhere in life simply because of the toxic environment they come from. You get home at the dinner table they are discussing other people's failures, " So and so dropped out of school" " So and so is working but we don't know what they do with money" So and so are getting divorced ". All that energy every evening makes you a negative person. Who spends more time worrying about what other people are doing instead of fixing yourself. I have friends that are always telling me the truth. Whenever I get to them they will be like " You need to fix this and that , you need to improve this and that " I go to bed and think how do I really fix this and that. I don't go bed thinking about other people's problems.

I think about my own problems. It's the environment surrounding me that is always encouraging me to be a better person. It's sad because in some families it's the mother who is even more toxic, you can't tell someone to ignore his mother but you can let here be aware that you no longer want to listen to such stories and why. Such tough economic times you need positive energy around you. Otherwise you might end up depressed. Two guys grew up together. Went to the same school and the same University. When they got to University one fell in love with the toil he decided to drop out one continued with his course until he graduated.

The one who dropped out had very little business experience his family disowned him. For year's and years he was moving from one toil to another with no luck. While the other friend got a job at the age of 24 he was earning R30000.00. His family was proud of him friends and neighbors respected him. Even people who were older than him called him uncle. The other friend was struggling. People kept asking why he dropped out because he was smart. At one point this guy was handing out pamphlets in the street trying to market his business. An ex school mate of his came to him and asked him" Is this why you dropped out? To handout fryers like a street kid what a waste".

He kept on hustling. He couldn't even attend family gatherings because he couldn't face his relatives and couldn't answer their questions. He moved out for two year's he wouldn't even visit home. He didn't know what he was going to say to his family he was hustling but things just didn't work out. His friend that he grew up with stopped talking to him when he got a job and according to the society he was doing well. At the age of 27 his friend got a promotion. The next month he upgraded and bought a R10000.00pm installment car.

Two months after buying the car he had an accident. The insurance couldn't pay because he was drunk. He was now paying R10000.00pm for a car he was not even driving. He bought another car on credit almost R20000.00 from his salary was going towards debt. Still drinking every weekend he made babies even. By the age of 36 he had babies from different women. Some he would take care off some he didn't. He had calls he was ignoring because of debt he was even thinking of quitting his jobs because of this.

His only hope was that he will get his pension fund one day and finally pay of his debt. The other friend who dropped out kept hustling at the age of 33 he got his first big contract at the mines. Trucks that will transport coal. The bank gave him a loan each truck would make him a profit of R100k a month. He then went on and build rooms that he would lease out to people also bought a few franchises. At the age of 37 the guy who got a job at 24 was in deep debt. The guy who was still broke at 24 until he hot his breakthrough at 37 was making R400kpm. Never compete with other people. Your parents will always discourage you when you go against the system because it has always protected them. Security comes first to them. Entrepreneurship is living a few years of your life like most people wont so that you live the rest of your life like most people can't. The guy dropped out and was seen as a failure dropped out. For more than 10 years he kept pushing lived like a street kid until one day his breakthrough came. Your breakthrough is coming be patient. Forget about the opinions of people who are not where you want to be. Only take advice from people who are where you want to be.

You can't take advice from someone who drives a Sportscar that he bought on credit when you want to own a paid up Lamborghini. Be brave. Bravery is the common denominator for all successful entrepreneurs. No risk no rewards.

When you decide to venture on this entrepreneurship journey the pressure from your parents might be almost unbearable. You can complete a degree and not find a job for 7 years but your parents will still be supportive of your career. Within 2 years of business your parents will start asking you.

Wheres the money ,? We don't see progress, where's your car? That time your still haven't made any profits yet your learning and breaking even but they don't understand. They see you busy but don't see you bringing anything at home. You borrow money every month to keep your business alive. Entrepreneurship is not a sprint it's a marathon. Allow your children to learn they might be powerful people in the future.

You only learn entrepreneurship from doing. The financially costly mistakes will teach you hard lessons. You need time to master the craft just like it takes 7 years for one to become a qualified medical doctor. You need years and experience to learn about business. The pressure we put on our kids who are into entrepreneurship is unnecessary.

Let them grow and learn. Give them time. The problem with this generation of entrepreneurs is we are so concerned with branding ourselves as successful entrepreneurs before we even become successful entrepreneurs. This now makes it hard for people to help us and for us to cut cost's and re-invest money into our businesses.

A guy wakes up in the morning wears a suit has R25 breakfast. Then takes pictures posts them captioning them "The toil or work hard", Whilst his doing nothing at all. Entrepreneurs today don't want to work they so concerned with being fancy. Someone who has a business that's not even making R5000 pm goes to radio and talks as if his a successful entrepreneur whilst his struggling his only got two suit's. The only problem with Faking it is that you even start believing it.

That's when you start having standards. You don't want to take a taxi anymore you don't want to drive a cheap car you don't want to start small. Because you've branded yourself as this big guy. In the old day's people started by driving taxis went all the way up and bought their own taxis. Some started by being street vendor's to owning supermarkets. You don't get that these day's everyone seems to be a big entrepreneur with empty pockets.

This causes a lot of confusion and depression at the same time. Keep it real. Grow slow. Fail forward. Someone from the rural areas. Told me how she used to hate Pizza when she first arrived in the City. Today she is addicted to it. Come to think of it. She has been eating healthy all her life in the rural areas. Healthy food from the soils no chemicals and organic meat. Besides that also the affordable lifestyle. What I've realized is that people in the city are living a life they really can't afford and even in the suburbs. When we were growing up we were told that people in the rural areas were not civilized and not educated. The more fluent you speak English the more civilized you are.

We wanted to take our children to private schools and let them forget their own history. In the long run this westernized lifestyle is killing us. We are struggling to keep up with it. An old man in the rural areas with one Van and a big Farm. Is wealthier than a man in the suburbs paying a bond and driving fancy cars while he has no other assets. Yet when this guy from the Suburbs comes to the rural areas he is celebrated. Even though he owns nothing intangible. I'm not saying it's wrong to live in the suburbs but to create wealth becomes extremely hard because of the lifestyle there.

It's too expensive look at all our soccer players who have died and left nothing behind. Fine you left a house in Sandton for your children to inherit. How will they maintain it? R15K plus for rates alone. My point is watch your finances build wealth first. There's too much pressure in these cities and majority of the population there is living fake lives.

What you see there is not what appears in their balance sheet. A person can be earning R300k monthly while his expenses are R350k, You get intimidated by such people.

When your mindset is poor you will always be poor no matter how much money you make. These success stories you see on Instagram most are a lie. On the ground creating wealth is a lie. Just think... Before you make any financial decisions. If your friend comes to you and says let us put together R5000 and import perfume and sell it.

You probably would not buy into that but If you see someone with a flashy life on social media saying his going to make you a millionaire in six months you throw in all your money.

Why is that? It's because people are lazy they also love hearing comfortable lies instead of the cold truth. At the end of the day, these people waste years and years of their careers looking for short cuts.

If you want success then you have to work for it, unfortunately, it will not happen over night you will first have to learn and fail many times before you even become successful. People don't want to hear the truth. If you're not willing to fail then go look for a job don't call yourself a risk taker if you're not willing to risk anything. When you're a beginner in business focus on learning and gathering experience, not money. Stop looking for quick solutions. Spoke to a guy yesterday. He earns a net of over R45k monthly. Lives below his means.

He is starting a business and plans to retire in the next 10 years. So I saw the quality of his equipment and asked him since his charging such a low price how is he going to make profit. He said" Look man, I don't care about profits , As long as I deliver quality service to my customers I'll be happy. For the next two years I'll be running at a loss of at least R20k monthly that R20k I'll be taking from my salary in five years I expect to be making R150k monthly profit. " So basically he is going to inject R20k monthly into his business to cover loses. When you have money business is easy but when your broke it's hard. Because you even get your pricing wrong because your not thinking about the quality of your service your thinking with your empty stomach.

This is why most businesses fail. This is why it's hard for small enterprises to compete with big companies. The lack of capital. Honestly speaking 90% of businesses fail in the first 6 months. The 10% survive but maybe 1% is profitable. You cannot open a business today and expect to have profits month end. Unless your doing something illegal. If the total monthly costs of running a business are R40000.00 to be on a safe side at least have R250k on the side to cover the loses. To avoid stress and panic month end. With this post I'm not discouraging people from starting businesses but I'm saying if your starting and your broke go for a business with less operational costs.

Don't just rent out a shop or an office when there's no back up plan. You can work from your home garage or streets or your friends place. Just minimize the risk until your profitable. The difficult thing about business is that you always have to save a lot for rainy days. Think about an Artist who was making R200k per week prior Covid who is now making R50k per week probably for the next 12 months. No matter how much you can be making in business you have to save for the rain days. There are those who are brave who don't save abo " Sobona khona" who spend everything they make. Those ones become homeless when shit hits the fan They are the ones who ask you to buy them beer then they tell you about their same old stories of how the use to enjoy life and spend money. Life is very short enjoy but in an affordable manner.

Think about the rainy days. Almost every business is unstable today it's tough. Be wise about your financial decisions. There's never been a good time to be called broke like today. You have a million excuses why. We need to come into terms with the reality that people will now live double lives with social media. In social media everyone is winning and happy but in reality people are losing jobs. Go to every bus stop in the morning see how many people are actually going to work. The youth is surviving because some of the parents are still working or a member of the family is working. We are broke and suffering. These dates your talking about we can't even afford them some people go the whole month without even getting a cent in their pockets.

My point is . Use social media productively forget what others are posting we are all going through a tough time just that some of us have become accustomed to living double lives. I'd love to see us discussing serious matters on social media like the high unemployment rate also depression and the high crime rate.

Instead of discussing thing's that won't put food in our stomach's like celebrity gossip. Let's discuss ideas. Some of you have became professional unpaid social media comedians some of you specialize in being critics. Use that platform to make money don't be a tool. You're starving at home and you're there wasting data on unnecessary things.

"You have to program your mind to think in terms of Assets over Liabilities"
- Obakeng Mosime

Chapter 3

BRUTAL TRUTHS EVERYONE NEEDS TO HEAR

Life is a journey full of challenges, and sometimes the best way to grow and learn is to face some brutal truths. In this chapter, I will share with you some brutal truths that every person needs to hear.

You are responsible for your life

The first brutal truth is that you are responsible for your life. You are the only one who can create the life you want. You cannot blame others for your failures or expect someone else to solve your problems. Take ownership of your life, and make the necessary changes to achieve your goals.

Failure is a necessary part of success

Another brutal truth is that failure is a necessary part of success. Every successful person has experienced failure. It is not a sign of weakness, but rather an opportunity to learn and grow. Embrace failure, learn from it, and use it as a stepping stone to success.

Time is your most valuable asset

Time is your most valuable asset. You cannot buy more time, and once it is gone, it is gone forever. Use your time wisely, and focus on what truly matters. Spend time with your loved ones, pursue your passions, and work towards your goals.

Success requires hard work

Success requires hard work. There are no shortcuts or magic pills to success. You need to put in the work, stay focused, and be persistent. Success is not a destination; it is a journey, and it requires consistent effort and dedication.

Your attitude determines your success

Your attitude determines your success. If you have a negative attitude, you will attract negative experiences and outcomes. On the other hand, if you have a positive attitude, you will attract positive experiences and outcomes. Your attitude is a choice, and you have the power to choose a positive mindset.

Change is necessary for growth

Change is necessary for growth. If you want to grow and achieve your goals, you need to be willing to change. This can be uncomfortable and even painful at times, but it is necessary for growth. Embrace change, and use it as an opportunity to learn and improve.

You cannot please everyone

You cannot please everyone. No matter what you do, there will always be someone who disagrees or criticizes you. Focus on what you believe in and what is important to you, and do not let others' opinions hold you back.

Your comfort zone is your enemy

Your comfort zone is your enemy. If you want to grow and achieve your goals, you need to step out of your comfort zone. This can be scary and uncomfortable, but it is necessary for growth. Push yourself out of your comfort zone, and embrace new challenges and opportunities.

You are capable of more than you think

You are capable of more than you think. Do not limit yourself based on your past experiences or current circumstances. Believe in yourself, and have faith in your abilities. You have the potential to achieve great things if you are willing to put in the work and stay focused.

Your health is your wealth

Your health is your wealth. Without good health, you cannot enjoy life or achieve your goals. Take care of your physical, mental, and emotional health, and prioritize self-care. Make healthy choices, exercise regularly, and take time to recharge.

Your health is your wealth. This is a well-known saying that holds a great deal of truth. While many of us may focus on achieving financial success or accumulating material possessions, the reality is that none of these things matter if we don't have our health.

The truth is that our health is the foundation upon which everything else is built. Without good health, we can't fully enjoy our lives, pursue our goals, or participate in the world around us. We might have all the money in the world, but if we're struggling with chronic illness or constantly battling pain or discomfort, that money won't mean much. In fact, poor health can actually be a drain on our finances. Medical bills, prescription medications, and lost income due to time off work can all add up, leaving us struggling to make ends meet. By contrast, good health can actually be a financial asset, allowing us to pursue our goals, be more productive at work, and enjoy a higher quality of life. But beyond the financial implications, good health is simply essential for living a happy and fulfilling life. When we're healthy, we have the energy and vitality we need to pursue our passions, connect with the people we love, and contribute to our communities. We feel better physically and mentally, which in turn allows us to be more engaged and active in all areas of our lives. So how can we prioritize our health and ensure that we're taking good care of ourselves?

The key is to focus on building healthy habits and taking a holistic approach to wellness. This means getting enough exercise, eating a healthy diet, getting enough rest, and managing stress effectively. It also means being proactive about our health by getting regular check-ups, staying up-to-date on preventative care like vaccinations and cancer screenings, and seeking medical attention when we need it. By being proactive about our health, we can catch potential health issues early and take steps to address them before they become more serious. Finally, it's important to remember that our health is not just about our physical bodies - it's also about our mental and emotional well-being.

This means taking steps to manage stress and cultivate a positive mindset, engaging in activities that bring us joy and fulfillment, and nurturing our relationships with loved ones. In the end, our health is truly our most valuable asset. Without it, we can't fully enjoy the other blessings in our lives, and we may even find ourselves struggling to get by. By prioritizing our health and taking a holistic approach to wellness, we can ensure that we're living our best lives, full of vitality, purpose, and joy.

In conclusion, these brutal truths may be difficult to hear, but they are necessary for growth and success. Embrace them, and use them as a road map to achieve your goals and create the life you want. Remember, life is a journey, and it is up to you to make it a great one.

Wishful thinking won't make you rich

You can have a million dollar business idea, but if you do not have a strategic plan on how you going to implement that idea, nothing will change, it will remain just an idea without purpose making it wishful thinking. Wishful thinking is a natural human tendency, and it can be tempting to rely on it as a means of achieving success. However, the truth is that wishful thinking alone won't get you very far. In order to truly achieve success, you need to take action and put in the hard work required to make your dreams a reality.

This means setting specific, measurable goals and developing a plan to achieve them, rather than simply hoping for the best and relying on luck or chance. One of the biggest problems with wishful thinking is that it can be incredibly passive. When we engage in wishful thinking, we often focus on the end result we want to achieve, rather than the steps we need to take to get there.

This can lead to a sense of complacency or inaction, as we wait for things to happen on their own rather than taking control of our own lives and making things happen. By contrast, successful people understand that they are in charge of their own destiny, and that achieving success requires consistent effort and hard work. They set clear goals for themselves, break those goals down into actionable steps, and then take consistent action towards achieving them. Another problem with wishful thinking is that it can be accompanied by a sense of entitlement.

When we engage in wishful thinking, we often believe that we deserve success simply because we want it. However, the reality is that success is not something that can be handed to us on a silver platter - it's something that we have to earn through our own efforts and actions.

Successful people understand this, and they're willing to put in the hard work and make the sacrifices required to achieve their goals. They don't expect success to be handed to them, and they don't waste time feeling sorry for themselves when things don't go their way. Instead, they pick themselves up, dust themselves off, and keep pushing forward towards their goals.

Ultimately, the key to success is to take action and to be willing to put in the hard work required to achieve your goals. Wishful thinking might provide a temporary sense of comfort or hope, but it won't actually get you any closer to where you want to be. Instead, focus on setting clear, specific goals, and then develop a plan to achieve them. Be willing to work hard, make sacrifices, and stay committed to your vision, even when things get tough.

Your obsession with finding happiness is what prevents its attainment.

Happiness is always present in your life. It's just a matter of connecting to it and allowing it to flow through you.

Donating money does less than donating time.

Giving your time is a way to change your perception and create a memory for yourself and others that will last forever.

When it comes to charitable giving, many people focus solely on donating money. However, while donating money is certainly important, donating time can often be even more impactful.

One of the main reasons for this is that donating time allows you to make a more direct and personal impact on the cause or organization you're supporting. When you donate money, it's easy to feel disconnected from the cause or to wonder where your money is actually going. By contrast, when you donate your time, you're able to see the immediate effects of your efforts and to form personal connections with the people you're helping.

Another benefit of donating time is that it often allows you to use your skills and expertise in a way that can be uniquely beneficial to the cause or organization. For example, if you're a lawyer, you might be able to provide pro bono legal services to a non-profit organization that supports victims of domestic violence. Or, if you're a graphic designer, you might be able to create marketing materials for a charity event. By using your skills and expertise in this way, you're able to make an even bigger impact than you would be able to through monetary donations alone.

In addition, donating time can be incredibly rewarding on a personal level. It allows you to feel like you're making a tangible difference in the world and to develop a sense of connection and purpose that can be difficult to achieve through other means. This can be especially true if you're able to work directly with the people or communities that you're helping, as it allows you to form meaningful relationships and to see firsthand the positive impact of your efforts. Of course, this isn't to say that donating money isn't important. Many non-profit organizations rely on financial donations in order to keep their operations running and to fund their programs and services. However, it's important to recognize that donating time can often be even more impactful than donating money.

If you're interested in donating time, there are many different ways to get involved. You might consider volunteering at a local charity or non-profit organization, donating your skills and expertise to a cause you're passionate about, or even starting your own fundraising campaign to support a cause you believe in. Whatever approach you choose, the key is to remember that donating time is just as important as donating money, if not more so. By getting involved in a hands-on way, you'll be able to make a direct and personal impact on the causes and communities you care about, and to experience the deep sense of fulfillment that comes from making a difference in the world.

You can't make everyone happy, and if you try, you'll end up losing yourself.

Stop trying to please, and start respect your values, and principles.

We all want to be liked and accepted by others, and there's nothing wrong with that. However, trying to make everyone happy is a recipe for disaster. Not only is it impossible to please everyone, but if you try, you'll end up losing yourself in the process.

When we try to please everyone, we end up sacrificing our own needs and values. We may compromise on our own beliefs or goals in order to make someone else happy, but in doing so, we're essentially giving away a part of ourselves. Over time, this can lead to a loss of self-identity and self-worth.

In addition to sacrificing our own needs, trying to make everyone happy is also a futile endeavor. No matter how hard we try, there will always be people who are unhappy with us or our decisions. This is simply a fact of life, and something that we need to accept. Furthermore, trying to please everyone can also lead to anxiety, stress, and burnout. It's an impossible task, and trying to keep everyone happy can leave us feeling overwhelmed and drained.

So, what's the solution? The solution is to focus on being true to yourself and your values, rather than trying to please everyone else. This means setting boundaries and saying no when something doesn't align with your goals or values, even if it means disappointing others. It also means accepting that not everyone will like or agree with you, and that's okay. We all have different perspectives and beliefs, and that's what makes us unique.

By embracing this, we can focus on building relationships with those who support and accept us for who we are, rather than trying to win over everyone. Finally, it's important to remember that you can't control how others feel or react. While it's natural to want to make others happy, ultimately their happiness is their responsibility, not yours. You can only control your own actions and reactions, so focus on being true to yourself and let go of the need to please everyone else. In conclusion, trying to make everyone happy is a losing battle that will only lead to sacrificing your own needs and values. Instead, focus on being true to yourself and your values, setting boundaries, and accepting that not everyone will agree or like you. By doing so, you can build relationships with those who support and accept you for who you are, and let go of the need to please everyone else. Remember, you can't make everyone happy, and if you try, you'll end up losing yourself in the process.

Your talent means nothing without consistent effort and practice.

Some of the most talented people in the world never move out out of their parent's house. It's often said that everyone has a talent, but simply having a talent is not enough to guarantee success. In fact, your talent means nothing without consistent effort and practice. Whether you're an athlete, musician, or artist, putting in the time and effort to hone your skills is essential if you want to achieve your full potential.

One of the biggest misconceptions about talent is that it's something you're born with. While it's true that some people may have a natural inclination towards a certain activity or skill, talent alone is not enough to ensure success. In fact, many talented individuals fail to achieve their goals simply because they don't put in the consistent effort and practice needed to succeed. Consistency is key when it comes to developing your talent. This means setting aside time each day or week to work on your craft, even when you don't feel like it or when other responsibilities are competing for your time. It also means being disciplined and focused during your practice sessions, rather than simply going through the motions. In addition to consistency, practice is essential if you want to develop your talent.

This means actively seeking out opportunities to practice and improve your skills, whether it's through attending classes, working with a coach or mentor, or simply practicing on your own. The more you practice, the more you'll develop the muscle memory and technique needed to perform at your best. Another important aspect of developing your talent is seeking out feedback and constructive criticism. While it can be difficult to hear feedback about your weaknesses or areas for improvement, it's essential if you want to continue growing and developing your skills. Seek out mentors or coaches who can offer honest and constructive feedback, and use that feedback to guide your practice and improvement. Ultimately, your talent means nothing without consistent effort and practice. While it's important to have a natural inclination towards a certain activity skill, talent alone is not enough to guarantee success.

It's only through consistent effort, discipline, and practice that you can develop your skills and achieve your full potential.

Nobody cares how difficult your life.

You are the author of your life's story. Stop looking for people to give you sympathy and start creating the life story you want to read. Life is full of ups and downs, and it's natural to experience difficulties along the way. However, it's important to understand that nobody cares how difficult your life is. This may seem like a harsh truth, but it's an important one to internalize if you want to lead a fulfilling and successful life.

The reality is that everyone has their own problems and challenges to deal with. While it's important to have a support system and people who care about you, it's not realistic to expect others to constantly sympathize with your struggles. Everyone is busy dealing with their own lives, and it's not fair to burden them with your problems. Furthermore, dwelling on how difficult your life is can lead to a victim mentality. When you constantly focus on your struggles and difficulties, you may start to feel helpless and powerless. This can lead to a mentality where you feel like a victim of your circumstances, rather than an empowered individual who can take control of their life. Instead of focusing on how difficult your life is, it's more productive to focus on what you can do to overcome your challenges. This means taking responsibility for your life and actively working towards your goals, even when things get tough.

It also means developing a growth mindset and embracing challenges as opportunities for learning and growth. It's important to remember that the challenges you face in life are not a reflection of your worth as a person. Everyone experiences setbacks and failures, and it's these experiences that can help you develop resilience and character. Instead of seeing difficulties as something to be ashamed of or hide from others, embrace them as a natural part of the human experience.

Ultimately, nobody cares how difficult your life is because they're too busy dealing with their own challenges. While it's important to seek support and advice from others, it's not fair to expect them to solve your problems for you. The key to overcoming difficulties is to take ownership of your life and actively work towards your goals, even when things get tough.

Investing in yourself isn't selfish.

It's the most worthwhile thing you can do. You have to put your own gas mask in order to save the person sitting right next to you. One of the most important investments you can make in your life is to invest in yourself. However, there is a common misconception that investing in yourself is selfish. In this statement, I will explain why investing in yourself is not selfish, but rather a necessary step towards personal and professional growth. Firstly, investing in yourself is not selfish because it benefits not only yourself, but also those around you. When you invest in your personal and professional growth, you become a better version of yourself. This means you can contribute more to your relationships, work, and community. By improving your skills, knowledge, and mindset, you can create positive change and inspire others to do the same. Secondly, investing in yourself is not selfish because it allows you to become self-sufficient.

When you invest in yourself, you become less dependent on others for your success and happiness. This means you can take control of your life and create the future you want. By investing in your personal and professional growth, you can develop the skills and mindset needed to overcome challenges and achieve your goals. Thirdly, investing in yourself is not selfish because it is a long-term investment. When you invest in yourself, you are making a commitment to your future.

This means you are willing to sacrifice short-term gratification for long-term success. By investing in your personal and professional growth, you can create a foundation for a fulfilling and prosperous life. Lastly, investing in yourself is not selfish because it is an act of self-love. When you invest in yourself, you are sending a message that you value yourself and your potential.

This means you are willing to prioritize your needs and well-being. By investing in your personal and professional growth, you can develop a positive self-image and increase your self-esteem. In conclusion, investing in yourself is not selfish, but rather a necessary step towards personal and professional growth. By improving your skills, knowledge, and mindset, you can create positive change and inspire others to do the same. You can become self-sufficient, take control of your life, and create the future you want. You can make a long-term investment in your future and develop a foundation for a fulfilling and prosperous life. And lastly, you can practice self-love and increase your self-esteem. So, do not hesitate to invest in yourself, because it is one of the best investments you can make in your life.

"You are the only one who can create the life you want"
– Obakeng Mosime

Chapter 4

THE ROLE OF ACTION IN ACHIEVING SUCCESS

Action is critical in achieving success. No matter how brilliant your ideas may be or how great your plans are, if you do not take action, they will remain just that – ideas and plans. Action is what turns your dreams into reality. When you take action, you bring your ideas to life, and this is what ultimately leads to success. In South Africa, there is a great need for action.

Many people have great ideas and plans, but they lack the initiative to take action. They are held back by fear, lack of resources, or a belief that they cannot make a difference. However, action is the key to overcoming these challenges and achieving success. If you want to make money, you need to become a master of persuasion. Persuasion is the art of getting people to say yes to your proposals, ideas, or offers. In this chapter, I will share with you my top tips on how to persuade effectively and make more money. Focus on solving problems.

The first rule of persuasion is to focus on solving problems. People buy products or services because they want to solve a problem or meet a need. Your job as a persuader is to identify these needs and offer a solution that meets them. To do this, you need to understand your target market and their needs. What problems do they face? What challenges do they need to overcome? What are their goals and aspirations? When you have a clear understanding of these, you can tailor your message to address their needs and offer a solution that meets them. Build credibility and trust People buy from people they like and trust. To persuade effectively, you need to build credibility and trust with your audience.

This can be achieved by demonstrating your expertise and knowledge, providing social proof, and building a relationship with your audience. Demonstrate your expertise by sharing your experience and credentials. This could be through your website, your marketing materials, or your interactions with your audience. Provide social proof by sharing testimonials, case studies, or success stories from satisfied customers. This helps to build trust and establish your credibility.

Use the power of emotions People make decisions based on emotions. To persuade effectively, you need to tap into the power of emotions. This can be achieved by using stories, metaphors, and vivid imagery to create an emotional connection with your audience. When you create an emotional connection, your audience is more likely to remember your message and take action. This can be a powerful tool in persuasion, as emotions can be used to create urgency, excitement, and a sense of belonging.

Use the power of language The words you use can have a powerful impact on persuasion. To persuade effectively, you need to use language that resonates with your audience and creates a sense of urgency or excitement. This can be achieved by using persuasive words, such as "limited time offer," "exclusive," "proven," or "guaranteed." In addition to using persuasive words, you should also avoid using negative or limiting language. This can include words like "can't," "won't," or "shouldn't." Instead, use positive language that focuses on solutions and benefits.

Use social proof social. It is a powerful tool in persuasion. People are more likely to follow the crowd and do what others are doing. To use social proof, you can provide testimonials, case studies, or success stories from satisfied customers. This can help to build trust and establish your credibility with your audience. Another way to use social proof is to show how many people have already taken advantage of your offer. This can create a sense of urgency and motivate your audience to take action.

Use scarcity. Scarcity is another powerful tool in persuasion. People are more likely to act when they believe something is in short supply or only available for a limited time. To use scarcity, you can offer limited-time discounts, exclusive deals, or a limited number of spots.

By creating a sense of urgency and scarcity, you can motivate your audience to take action and make a purchase. Accountability is what will heal you. It starts from simple things like saying you cut yourself with a Knife and not say a knife cut you. An object doesn't move itself.

Most of the suffering and discomforts We have come from what we invited. It's only when you get physically harmed by another person where you have no control over the pain you are to experience. But when you invest into a situation or a person with your heart and mind, You are to blame for everything that happens afterwards. If you date someone and feel betrayed, Ask yourself who put you in that position in the first place to agree to date that person. If you are unhappy about the people you surrounded by, Again ask yourself who is to blame for the food you cooked if it ends up too salty. There's absolutely nothing wrong that you don't have your life together in your 20s. You are thinking way ahead of your age because early maturity makes you want to be a problem solver. A generational curse breaker. You are already winning with the fact that you are identifying things most people see at old age. It a blessing to be stressed about seeking resources to be responsible. The problem is a person with no idea of what responsibility is. You are already winning if you see problems that need solving.

Unlike a person with resources but has no clue how to make progress of them. You are young and got chances to fail. If you are seriously interested in becoming financially independent and you have not yet acted on the preceding ideas, I would strongly recommend you do so now. For to continue on the next chapter without having done so, would be comparable to leaving on your journey with your car firing on only half its cylinders.

You can be almost certain that your automobile will break down, preventing you from reaching your desired destination. But by making certain that everything is properly tuned up, you can relax and adopt a calm, serene attitude, knowing that will get to your destination; and you will certainly be able to enjoy the scenery along the way!

Action is what turns your dreams into reality
– Obakeng Mosime

Chapter 5

SPIRITUAL MEANING BOOSTS SUCCESS

Years back , In the chilly month of December, I fondly recall an evening spent imbibing with my cousins. As the drinks flowed, we found ourselves in need of replenishment and thus embarked on a trip to the local shops. As we made our way out, a throng of revelers greeted us, and I was presented with opportunity to ride in various vehicles.

It was then that I made the choice to join a wealthy gentleman in his car, seeking to experience a different kind of aura. My kin viewed my decision as folly, unable to comprehend my reasoning. However, I knew that money possesses a particular energy, just as poverty does. Surround yourself solely with destitution, and it shall consume you. Dine, drink, and converse with the wealthy, and their energy shall imbue you with a spirit of affluence. A serene, placid energy permeates the realm of money, in stark contrast to the tumultuous din found in the realm of poverty Money exudes a tranquil demeanor, one that is altogether peaceful and calm. Spirituality is a deeply personal and subjective concept that can mean different things to different people. At its core, however, spirituality refers to the connection between individuals and something larger than themselves, whether that be a higher power, nature, or the universe as a whole.

Many people believe that cultivating a sense of spirituality can have a positive impact on their personal and professional success, leading to greater happiness, fulfillment, and purpose in life. We will explore how spirituality can affect your success and provide practical advice and examples for implementing spiritual practices in everyday life.

One of the ways that spirituality can impact success is by helping individuals to develop a sense of purpose and meaning in their lives. When individuals feel connected to something larger than themselves, they may be more motivated to pursue goals that align with their values and beliefs. This can lead to greater focus, drive, and persistence in the pursuit of success. For example, a person who feels called to serve others may find fulfillment and success in a career that allows them to make a positive impact on the world. Another way that spirituality can affect success is by promoting inner peace and well-being. Many spiritual practices, such as meditation, prayer, or mindfulness, can help individuals to quiet their minds, reduce stress, and cultivate a sense of calm and tranquility. This can improve mental health and well-being, making individuals better equipped to handle the challenges and setbacks that may arise on the path to success. Spirituality can also promote positive relationships with others, which can be important for success in both personal and professional contexts.

Many spiritual traditions emphasize the importance of treating others with compassion, kindness, and respect. When individuals embody these qualities in their interactions with others, they may be more likely to build strong and supportive relationships that can help them to achieve their goals. For example, a business leader who treats their employees with respect and empathy may be more likely to inspire loyalty and commitment among their team members, leading to greater success for the organization as a whole.

In order to implement spiritual practices in everyday life, it is important to first develop a clear understanding of what spirituality means to you. This may involve exploring different spiritual traditions, reflecting on your own beliefs and values, or seeking guidance from a spiritual mentor or community. Once you have a solid foundation in your spiritual practice, you can begin to incorporate it into your daily routine in a way that feels authentic and meaningful to you. One practical way to cultivate spirituality in everyday life is through meditation or mindfulness practices. These practices involve focusing your attention on the present moment, often through the use of breathing techniques or visualization exercises.

Meditation can help to calm the mind, reduce stress, and promote feelings of inner peace and well-being. It can also help to develop greater self-awareness and insight, which can be useful for identifying areas of your life where you may be feeling unfulfilled or disconnected from your values. Another way to incorporate spirituality into your daily routine is through acts of service or generosity. Many spiritual traditions emphasize the importance of helping others and making a positive impact on the world. This can involve volunteering your time and talents to a charitable organization, donating to a cause you care about, or simply being kind and compassionate to those around you.

By practicing generosity and service, you can cultivate a sense of purpose and meaning in your life while also making a positive impact on others. Learn to build with people that want to go forward. Learn to network with people that are already making moves in life. It's useless to get lost in politics about land and blacks working Together to build Heaven On Earth because we all know how our people are. If you get the opportunity to work with people outside your hood. Your culture and your race. Do that quickly. It's useless to force matters. Africa is a place where nothing changes. If you want improvement. Avoid people that are stuck. Dead ideas will cost you. Move with those that are moving. Build with those that are building.

There's no Entity that will come and save our continent. Save yourself. Forget everything that isn't moving and move with people that are serious. Art is being creative. The mistake people make is to think art is about using pens to draw. Art is any form of creativity. People in love are artistic. That's why some couples stand out from others. Get admired more than others. It's an indication that you have two creative people that have combined their energies.

Their every action is attractive because it comes from being creative. With this calls for the two souls to have love that is active. Energy of attraction that is constant. When love is one sided or non existent, people see it ugly. Criticize it more than admiring it. Love somebody that decorates you. It's not out of privilege. But, you can't be comfortable in your 20s, The age where you should be learning independence, to be still asking for Data, Clothes, Takeaways and pocket money from your parents and siblings that wake up to toil while you have pride telling yourself not to toil in certain ways because you got a degree or you are too cute and famous on Instagram to sweep the roads. You got the energy to be having sex which will potentially make you a parent but you have no plan of providing.

The responsibility carried by parents right now will be on our shoulders tomorrow when we are the new adults in our homes. That weed you smoke all day, Those naked pictures you post on social media for Likes won't make you mature to head the family culturally, spiritually, financially and socially. Look at yourself in the mirror, You are the next Husband Or Wife but the only thing you are a Professional in is arranging a Hubbly, rolling a blunt and mixing vodka NeDash. It's a shame.

When you put liquid in the freezer, It changes to ice. The transition here is due to time. It's the basic law of time that when it is involved, anything exposed to it is bound to undergo change. Liquid under prolonged exposure to cold temperature becomes ice. You don't see this as a loss for water to lose it's liquid form to ice because you have no emotions attached to the whole process. But when it comes to you, with emotions involved, you declare change as loss.

You don't see the significance of living life with the experience of having no parents. with the realization that in love sometimes things won't go your way. There's different capabilities ice has that liquid doesn't But as humans, the limitation of seeing change as loss is the reason many choose not to embrace growth from painful situations. But instead use the lack of strength as an excuse to cause pain to others. You may been born soft as liquid but be aware you have to make use of life even when it turns you to ice. Put feelings aside and use logic. We create our own luck. What you calling as blessings.

Work of the Ancestors. God. Is all your good actions under any circumstance playing themselves onto your favor. Prayer and any form of aligning your energy for good rewards is just setting your alignment for what you had already done to quickly come back at you.

Don't become too entitled, It will create unrealistic expectations and ruin the life experience for you. Just because you a virgin or didn't sleep around much doesn't automatically mean you deserve marriage. Just because you not killing and stealing for money doesn't mean life should easily bless you with money from your clean toils. You can still be played even if you not a player.

Entitlement is a disability. Right now there's serious competition for resources and some people want a red carpet rolled down for them by the government. It may be mother nature but this is not your mother's house. Men who don't kill still get robbed and shot. Women who don't wear revealing clothes still get raped. prepare for what life gives and deal with it.

Things don't happen straightforward in this world. If you are putting no effort to produce what you eat, give it a few years and you will start considering the animals you are kicking away from your doorstep. When food prices go up, chasing money is exactly the route to the mouse trap they want you to take because it will strip you off the Godly way of existing. You consider crime, being a sellout and a whole bunch of other things that will terrorize other humans just for you to sleep fed.

A lot of people would be comfortably unemployed if they had the natural capability of growing food. Being taught at a young age is beneficial, being taught in adulthood doesn't mean you are late. What matters is starting. Come join us in this garden preparation month. All you need is a backyard and passion. You don't wait until you rich to help the poor. You don't wait until you are married to start loving wholeheartedly.

You don't wait until the mother or father of your child contributes in your child's life before you become a loving parent too. You don't start being humble when life has knocked you down. You don's start believing in prayer when you are suffering. Goodness shouldn't come from you when you feel you have to give and expect something in return. Our comfort in life is more determined by the energy we put out to the universe than the reactions of people. So do according to what feels right at the time. life will reward you much better. Whether a person is spiritual, rich, poor or beautiful, the one thing we all have as humans is jealousy. Nobody is spared from it no matter how humble we may be. But here's the difference. Jealousy is what rises when someone achieves something in line with our desires but what separates our reactions is what we choose this jealousy to awake within us. For some it brings inspiration where we get motivated to learn how the other person did it. Be happy for them. And then you find those who develop hate within them.

When other people's achievements make them wish they can lose them all so they can be the same at the bottom level. That's the road you shouldn't take. It's not about what you feel. It's about what comes out as a result of that feeling. Focus on what you want and don't try to tell the universe how to get It. That's a bigger dimension out of your hands. You may think you want a good man or a good woman where you live but the universe may bring a job that's in another province and you find a partner there appropriate for you. At the end you get what you desire, but it doesn't come how you imagined. You may desire independence but be fearful and then life just takes away your

It may come in a way that' not polite but guess what, you still get that independence. I repeat. Focus on what you want and don't just imagine how you are going to get it. It won't work that way. When you start waking up a minute before your alarm rings, It means you are aligned. An alarm is set by you to ring at a particular time of the day. That whole alignment goes with the universe. When you are in sync, your energies know when to wake up without the alarm or soon before it can make noise. This physical alignment is also present spiritually. You don't start coming across enlightened people by mistake. There's an alarm for your spiritual body. Some people only see posts about Sex, alcohol etc all day. It's not by mistake that you see posts that are calling you to grow. It's time to let go of your fears.

If you don't care about your goals, nobody else will
– Obakeng Mosime

Chapter 6

PRACTICAL WAYS TO MAKE MONEY

This is for individuals 'ko Kasi' (at townships) but applies literally to everyone that want to achieve success. I am going to provide you with ideas and simple steps to follow. Whether you follow the steps or not it's really your choice, I still sleep better at night regardless.

Collect cans.

Aluminum cans are the most sustainable beverage package on virtually every measure. Aluminum cans have higher recycling rate and more recycled content than competing package types. They are lightweight, stack-able and strong, allowing brands to package and transport more beverages using less material. Aluminum can are far more valuable than plastic or glass material. Helping make municipal recycling programs, financially viable and effectively subsidizing the recycling of less valuable materials in the bin. If you collect 2000 cans a week you can make around R6000.00 per month. You can go to parks where people consume beverages every weekend, go to pubs, dumping sites, schools etc. What you need to do is build a relationship with people. Ask to put your bin strategically at the back of of a restaurant and at clubs where they only put cans in those bins. Negotiate them a share of your profit. Even if you collect 60 cans a day that's around R2000.00 a month in your pocket, way better than waiting for the government to give you R350.00 a month.

This is a business you can start tomorrow with Zero capital. You can take your cans to : Collect a can , just check for the nearest one in your area. All you need is R100 per day income. Of course, as with any business opportunity, there are risks and challenges to be aware of. However, the key to success is to focus on the positive, and to look for the one reason why this opportunity will work. By employing a strong, determined mindset and a focus on sustainability and community, it is possible to build a successful business while contributing to a more sustainable future.

Flea Market

Flea markets are a popular destination for shoppers looking for unique and interesting items, and for sellers looking to connect with buyers and make a profit. A flea market is typically a marketplace that offers a variety of goods, including antiques, collectibles, handmade crafts, vintage clothing, and more. Flea markets can be found in many cities and towns, and are often held in open-air settings such as parking lots, fields, or other public spaces. One of the key advantages of flea markets is the opportunity to find items that are not available in traditional retail stores.

This can include one-of-a-kind vintage items, handcrafted goods, and unique collectibles. For shoppers, the experience of browsing through the various stalls and vendors can be exciting and rewarding, as they discover new treasures and hidden gems. For sellers, flea markets offer a chance to connect with buyers directly and make a profit by selling their goods. Many vendors at flea markets are small business owners or individuals looking to make some extra money by selling items they have collected or created. Flea markets also provide a platform for artists and craftspeople to showcase their work and build a customer base.

In addition to the shopping and selling opportunities, flea markets can also be a social gathering place for the community. Many flea markets have a festive atmosphere, with food vendors, live music, and other entertainment. For some people, attending a flea market is a weekend tradition, a chance to catch up with friends and neighbors, and enjoy a fun day out. People take the idea of selling clothes at the flea market for granted. Some people make R3000.00 a week through this business or R12000.00 a month. Some of our graduates are being exploited in internships, we are facing tough economic times, businesses like this can help us survive. What most people normally do is Buy 200 units of dresses for R1500.00 and sell them for R30 each making R4500.00 profit from 200 units.

Sneaker Wash

This is one of the most underrated businesses you can start and make decent profits. People are lazy and that can be an advantage to you, an opportunity to exploit their laziness. This business requires less than R600.00 to start, Air brushes price ranges from as little as R250.00 and the sprays from R50.00. You can even start with your normal brush and soap. 10 sneakers a day at R30.00 each pair is R300.00 daily revenue. If you're going to be using sprays you'd have to charge more but the process will be much quicker. This is one business you can overlook that could earn you R9000.00 a month. Don't wait for people from across the border to come and take advantage of this opportunity. If I was you I'd go on YouTube and find out what the perfect sprays are on Google to get proper prices. Tomorrow I would create a page, Next week I would start my sneaker wash business. Simply because I'm tired of being broke and depressed. Your future is literally on your hands. Hot-dogs Business opportunity you can start with a small capital or even R350.00 that the government is giving to people as unemployment grants.

Sell hot dogs at school. Let's say you sell each hot dog for R10.00 and each day you sell 30 units. R10.00 x 30 hot dogs = R300.00 per day R300.00 x 5 days = R1500.00 per week R1500.00 x 4 = R6000 per month. You can even make more if you decide to sell at hospitals or home affairs as there are hundreds of people (potential clients) who are going in and out per hour. Complaining is not a strategy, if you want to truly change your situation, stop wasting time complaining and start fixing things.

Sometimes, what we are looking for is just in front of us. Growth comes from finding opportunities in problems. Think beyond your circumstances, you can overcome everything. I think it's time for the South African youth to go back to the drawing board.

We need to learn something called survival without a job. You can't be waiting on the government to give you a job for 10 years, instead figure out a way you can survive and earn a living without waiting for someone to employ you. Get out of your comfort zone. Start small, you can even start a car wash for R50.00 a car. 6 cars a day make for you in a month R9000.00 revenue a month. Save that money and live cheap, don't buy unnecessary things. Next step, buy affordable piece of land and build a 2 room house if you can. Keep growing from there, grow your small business, in 3 years you might be making R30 000.00 per month. Those are the skills we need right now, just cut off that luxury life and focus, write a plan step by step and just follow those steps.

Have a plan for your future, this is why the wealthiest people have journals and schedules that they follow everyday, they don't skip an important meeting that's going to contribute towards their wealth just because they don't feel like attending that particular meeting. Don't be a Doer don't be a Dont'er That's my favorite quotes from my favorite movie titled 'No pain no gain'.

People know very well about investing. It's just investing money that they don't like. Because people don't like money. They like what money can buy. That's why they spend faster than they can invest. People that like money find pleasure in seeing it grow. People that like things surround themselves with people who can afford those things. They enjoy a millionaire spending money on them at a club but nobody will stop to ask him how he makes money. They take pictures of a rich person just to post. But will never run up to that person to ask how they make money multiply. I can bet with my life that the majority of people keep screenshots of expensive trips and accessories that they would spend on if they became millionaires but zero screenshots of mind maps that can multiply their income to actually be millionaires.

There's nothing new under the sun. Everything you want to achieve has been done before. You want to achieve this or that, you want to make your first million, you want to manufacture your own cleaning detergents, you want to be a property mogul, there's already a blueprint for that. All you have to do is check history. If it's not broken why fix it.

Get inspiration and do it your way but in the end the satisfaction is the same. So if you think your dreams are impossible enough to achieve think again. Your dreams already there and probably achieved by someone and waiting to be achieved by you this time. There's a guy I know who decided to invest in a trampoline for R1500.00. On the first day he made R70.00 by charging kids R2.00 to use it for 5 minutes. This shows that there's money at Kasi (rural areas) and everywhere else, don't let them lie to you. All you need is to spot a busy area and start a business like that. The goal is to have multiple streams of income by all means. Those R2's goes a long way when you count them. Is that is needed is to take action.

Think big but start small. The small businesses will fund your initial dream and get you to the level you want to achieve. Offer a service – any service (like delivery, laundry, copywriting. But instead of buying the cars, the washing machines, or paying the office rent, you actually use the services of decent and reliable small businesses who already offer services, but have no recognizable brand and serve only a very limited reach. Add something unique to the services they offer- you could be the fastest service in town for example. Build a network of small businesses.

You are really just coordinating the process, but you have a wide outreach this way, and your network can act fast because you give the job to the one that delivers in time. This way you get jobs to these small businesses while building your own company and brand. Fastest in town and 24 hours per day? Your customers will love it. There are many more efficient and creative ways you can use to start your business on a shoe string budget.

The most important point in our view is that you do not let the world pass by and the competition build up while you are still looking for capital. Besides, many who finally managed to get the 'big money' together they were desperately looking for often face sudden cash flow problems along the way. Thousands and thousands of start-up business fail despite the initial start-up capital raised, leaving a lot of people in debt or with little motivation to start all over again. Yes, access to capital can give your business a head start or may be necessary to grow your business at one point.

Interested in developing a food brand, a home-made recipe or an organic beauty product? Start it in your own kitchen, perfect your product, let family and colleagues try it. Make improvements where necessary, get some very cheap (but still smart looking) packaging, put a sticker with your brand on it. Produce 100 units and pay for a very small stand or desk at the taxi rank or the mall or even at the complex. You can also use your own product and establish a network of individual sellers for your product who earn a commission for each item they sell for you to their friends, colleagues, neighbours and customers. This way, you are not relying on supermarkets for example to buy from you and you don't have to do all the selling yourself, if it is mostly done by others.

"There's nothing new under the sun, Everything you want to achieve has been done before."
– Obakeng Mosime

Chapter 7

BUILD MULTIPLE STREAMS OF INCOME

Have you ever found yourself struggling to make ends meet? Maybe you're working a full-time job, but the paycheck just isn't enough. Or perhaps you're a freelancer, and you're tired of the feast or famine cycle that comes with that lifestyle. Whatever the case may be, the idea of building multiple streams of income has probably crossed your mind at some point. And you're not alone. Many people are turning to side toils and passive income streams to supplement their main source of income.

Let's be real, working a 9-5 job and relying solely on one paycheck is so last century. Life is unpredictable, and having only one source of income is like trying to cross a tightrope without a safety net. You never know when you might fall. Building multiple streams of income gives you the freedom and security to pursue your passions without constantly worrying about finances. Plus, it's just plain smart.

So your going to sit at home. Take selfies with filters all day long while other kids are selling tea, weaves, yellow containers on social media then you expect a guy to take care of you? How can I take care of an adult with two legs, two hand's a heart lungs and a full functioning brain? Must buy nails, hair, clothes take you out on dates while you on the side your busy faking your life. You have pride. Your lazy. It's only rich people who can do that. Most people still have to look after their families and pay their own bill's.

It's a struggle being a middle-class South African and still some people want to add salt in our wounds. Laziness must fall. Go to YouTube search for ways of making money online go to Google like and follow all business pages on Instagram and Facebook find out what other people are doing be active. Use your data effectively.

You're busy being a comedian on Facebook while people are marketing their business and next thing you ask them for money. That's not fair at all. I know with all this anxiety caused by inflation, the pandemic, unemployment and everything that is happening. A lot of people are struggling to sleep. To keep yourself busy at night. At least find an online job you can work at night. Find an online toil. Learn a new language. Learn a new skill. You can even learn skills like plumbing, mechanics, electronics etc. Online Telkom sells monthly night data of 100gb for R100.00 that data can come into good use. You don't do anything during the day then set an alarm wake up at 12am and toil and sleep in the morning. It's quiet. The best time to work and make money while everyone is sleeping.

People who have given up or lost faith are dead they just waiting for their date to be buried. Never die while your still breathing. Never lose faith. Keep fighting till the end. Theres always a way forward even baby steps count. The level of inequality is too high. It's time for you to reach a standpoint. Where you say this is me. I can't go out on weekends anymore no more hanging out with friends who have it all together. It's time for me to fight for my financial freedom whether I wash peoples cars or clean yards or houses or sell fat cookies.

Bank accounts don't lie. Most of us black youth are just caught up in the mix. Some people think they made it because they are surrounded by people who have made it or maybe they dating people who have made it. Look at yourself in the mirror check your bank balance and your statements for the past six months that's actually you. The danger here in South Africa is the high inequality. It makes others think they are something also the degrees. In a country with a 0 economic growth a degree won't guarantee you success. You need to toil. We have street vendors who take care of their children.

We have graduates who can't even buy milk for their children because they are being exploited by big companies. You need to be both book and street smart. Look at the opportunities around you. These jokes bring shared on socials, the entertainment on TV they trying to make us forget the current economic crises we are in. Just a few days I had a conversation with an old lady. She said. "You know homeless people have it easy. They eat 4 times a day. The get food from different donors, us who are staying in flat we are starving", Which is true there's too much hidden poverty in this country. Don't fake it. You need to look at yourself in the mirror otherwise you will be fooled by the society. Things like Durban July fool us into thinking blacks are getting richer.

The fact is the masses of black people are actually getting poorer. One working person in the house has to carry the whole house hold. The masses are ignorant today. We can't fight in unity like we did fighting apartheid. It's one man for himself. If your not discussing the high unemployment rate, the retrenchments, the rand versus the dollar, new business opportunities etc. With your lifetime partner than what are you discussing? Be with someone whom you can at least have a decent conversation with about social and economical issues. Some people don't even know what's happening in this world yet they love the finer things. It's like they moving in the opposite direction. Living in their own planet. Move to rural areas farm your own cows and chicken for meat. Plant your own food. It's no use at all staying in the suburbs where everything is overpriced especially the rate's. You can buy a big piece of land in the rural areas and build a big house for you and your family get a piece of mind.

It's better then staying in a busy city and having sleepless night's because of debts and rates too many expenses. It's no use for us being slaves to money just because we want to maintain specific standards put there by the society. Accept your situation and build from it. Most of the people in the suburbs are killed by stress. Majority die poor. There are cheaper ways of doing thing's be smart.

The age of worrying about what other people will think about us is over its time for us to face reality. Everyone needs to have multiple streams of income, even the world's wealthiest people keep accumulating more wealth simply because they understand the importance of diversification and creating multiple streams of income for the future of their great grandchildren. Wake up and focus. You have to do different like the few to get what the majority don't have. It won't just simply come. we have a small percentage of millionaires and billionaires because they think and do different with money.

We have couples that manage to stay together even after a baby is involved because they adjust to the new form of the relationship. We have a few emotional and mental stable people because they do different everyday. A lot of people having it difficult in this life expect to have comfort using hard material. They are aggressive to their partners while expecting a soft touch from them. They treat money like a virus that has to quickly leave their bank accounts but complain for having no money. They expect to find happiness by causing misery to others which is all just the wrong formula for success. Networking makes life easier. It's not a sign of being weak. When you have no onion, getting it from your neighbour is networking. Getting referred to a company when seeking for a tender or employment is networking. Ask people for their numbers if you think they can be useful to you. One way or the other we need each other.

There no individual success. There are people who know better ways to win soccer bets. To get through depression. Who know more about investing.

There's always an easier way to get what you are struggling to achieve. Some will be uninterested in mixing with you but some will open the door for you. Just ask around. Your network is your net-worth.

Having only one source of income is like trying to cross a tightrope without a safety net, you never know when you might fall
– Obakeng Mosime

Chapter 8

AWAKENING

Here is an example of how the world works. Let's say There are 10 people in the room. 1 person sells bread, the second person sells meat, and the third person sells spices. The rest of the people in the room are unemployed. So that's 7 unemployed people and only 3 business people. Let's take money from the business people and give the unemployed people 200 Rands each. So all the unemployed people have been given the same amount. Do you know that after a while, all that money will go back to the business owners? Why? Because the business owners have somethings those 7 people do not have. The business owners have assets. Assets will always put money in your pocket.

If everybody in the world was given a million. Those same millions will sooner or later go back to business owners. Go back to the same companies that were already rich. That is how the system was designed. That's why our neighborhoods as black people don't change. White people give you your salary knowing very well that you will spend that same salary in their malls, shopping centres, and their businesses. No matter how much they give you. It will always come back to them because you have no assets. Whatever you do. Make sure you have an income. Make sure you have something that brings in money. Even if you are making R100 a day. That's R700 a week. Small money becomes big money.

Too many people left their jobs because of small money. Too many people stopped hustling because of small money not realizing that small money is better than no money. A person selling potatoes on the street is richer than an unemployed graduate. A person washing cars is better than a graduate. Anybody that is getting money will always be better than nothing. Learn to swallow your pride, you are getting old. I can attest that I personally went through this same situation. I had a decent job at one of the retail stores working as a supervisor and I just left the job because small money, feeling like the company didn't see my worth. But let me tell you something for free. Everybody can be replaced! There's always someone out there working harder than you, hungrier, more passionate, more invested than you. So do not make the mistake of thinking you can't be replaced. Long story short I left the job and couldn't find a job for years after that. If I knew what I know now I would have made better choices. Don't be that guy. Do not find yourself In this situation whereby you will be drained by sadness and confused with regret. Success is a choice. Drugs are increasingly being used not because of those who make them. It's not about the supply. It's mainly about how unaware people are becoming when it comes to solving inward problems.

They are increasingly having an outward perception of approaching life. That's why when you talk about the Aura, Chakras, 4 different types of bodies, 3rd Eye, Consciousness and see people having confused faces. This outward perception of life is the reason you see people investing more on looking good instead of first being good people. You shouldn't get angry when you warn someone about the use of alcohol, smoking, spending too much, sleeping around, abandoning their child and any other act that is a temporary solution to a long term emotional or mental issue.

An advice that comes from a good place should leave you with an awareness that they may decline It and therefore should be left to face the consequences. Resorting to anger is an indication that you are letting other peoples choices reflect your standard of being. You want to live of them. You have to let people fail without holding yourself accountable. At the end of the day we all gonna answer for our own faults and ignorance. When a road is being built and constructors get to a river, They don't put a wall to stop the water so they can continue with the same road. They build a bridge. Because they already aware that overtime the water will break the wall.

I've had a lot of people asking how can they control their thoughts to get through misery. What they don't know is nobody controls the mind under a situation where it is flooded with painful possibilities and things that didn't happen just for you to hurt more. That's why it is always advised that you find something so distract you. could be Gym. Washing. Cleaning The whole point is to build a bridge until that river of bad thoughts dries up.

You realize how you get over a breakup when you start having friends over to talk about other things. The mind cannot be controlled. It needs to be distracted. Money is not an excuse for life to be soft on you. Karma can't be bought. Life just serves you based on who you are. There are rich couples that can't have babies. But there are couples financially incapable who are producing babies by the dozens. This is one of the indications that we don't bring anyone to life. Life comes through us.

The most expensive medical assistance fail to get a couple pregnant while contraceptives also fail to prevent life from coming to existence. The sooner you become aware that you have zero control over what you going face in this life but total control over how you handle the matter, is the better you going to prepare without using the mindset of being a victim because it will delay you from growth. If you need something done perfectly do not delegate. Do it yourself. There's a lot of noise on social media as to what's best in a relationship. What a real woman is. What a real man is. I'm not saying don't take some of the advice given, But develop the mindset of scaling whether the advice given is in sync with what your relationship really demands.

Nobody knows your partner better than you. You come across convincing posts that may plant a seed of confusion in you to start thinking your partner is slower financially. Not so beautiful or exciting. But remember that all couples that are celebrating aren't celebrating the same fruits from a tree that you are watering. Some are celebrating less drama. financial breakthrough. a baby. A restored connection. So understand the tree you are watering with your partner before you start thinking of cutting it.

You are witnessing less weddings in the black community, not because blacks are not in love, but the economic wave is drowning them. They are not surfing it. Majority of blacks get paid R10k going down and if look at that, you ask yourself how is it going to be possible to pay for an apartment, groceries, transport, school fees, wedding, medical aid, invest and still afford relief activities from the workload on weekends. Our parents did it because inflation wasn't this hectic, they got RDP's. Look at you, there's a very high chance you'll live in your parents house until old age if you don't look for other income sources besides employment. We lose a true purpose of unity and live for materialism so capitalism can flourish for those who made the system. The sad part is you'll notice men are getting into groups, learning about financial literacy while women are shifting further into the space of being consumers. That's why so many men are under pressure to make money while giving their women the finer things that they see everyday from social media platforms.

This is like moving one step forward and taking 3 steps back because you can't invest while spending more to that liability that only tells you about money when there's something you have to spend on. Don't be comfortable with the reality of your woman lacking financial intelligence because that's where your downfall is, slowly but surely. It's different things that happen in a man and a woman's head when they don't have money. Women know they can be broke because they will still have access to the things they want later. That's why a woman will spend all her money fast as soon as she finds out she's get the money she's spending from you. But with men it's different. Men feel out of place when they are broke not because their manhood is attached to money, but it's because everyone runs to the man when there's a need for money. And since the nature of a man is on providing, It adds weight of stress and discomfort when tools to provide are not there. Children run to their fathers. Women run to their men. Mothers run to their sons when the father isn't there. Men run to nobody. If women are in it to build with men, They should know that a man already feels down for being broke, Insulting him is adding fuel to the fire. Instead you can help him think of ways to get that money because a stable minded man will get money to give it so his family.

Listening to yourself think seems like torture because that's where realization about your own nature comes. How do you listen to yourself think? Ever notice how you just turn on the television when you are sitting alone and not even watch it? Open TikTok but scroll non stop without focusing on it? That's how you run away from having silence in your space because silence activates the voice in you to speak. It activates guilt. It may remind you of how selfish you are. How much of a coward you are. How controlling you are. It's only a few people that know how to sit in silence and embrace it.

Those who don't use the television or the phone to create a distraction will use the memory part of the mind and think of all the negative ways to torture themselves into depression. You end up victimizing yourself just so you can avoid self realization. The data you really need is not the one to browse through different social platforms and streaming sites smoothly without any buffering. The data you really need is of knowledge. On how you can browse through your emotions, thoughts to your spiritual self without buffering halfway on why people don't like you. On how much of a failure you are.

Ever notice when you thinking of solutions and you just get caught up on a problem to pin yourself down and be depressed?! That's the real buffering you need to work on. Good internet data is not the only important thing to get. Also get that data to improve yourself internally. Quit trying to make every effort to make other people comfortable and happy all the time. While you think it makes you a good person, It's actually sucking life and happiness out of you. You are exactly like a drip at the hospital. Once the plastic is empty, You can be replaced and life will keep going for the patient. Be a little selfish. There's nothing wrong with that.

In a community that fears poverty more than attaining stable behavioral structures, Money becomes the dominant resource and not human values. Which means people lose the significance of marriage. Being a family building union. But instead becomes a way to escape poverty. Guns no longer be about protection, but become weapons of absorbing a portion of wealth from the haves. Education loses its foundation of being an aspect of learning but becomes a factory to manufacture slaves and not intelligent beings. When every expectation revolves around how people can escape poverty more than the foundation principles of unity, expect betrayal, distrust and false promises. Money is an enhancing tool. If you are toxic without it, you will be further toxic with it. You feel deeper relaxation when you go to rural areas, mountains and bushes simply because of one thing. Less contamination.

Wherever you walk upon as a human you leave an imprint, a portion of your energy. The places I just mentioned usually don't have many people dwelling on them so the landmark stays less contaminated. In the city you find even at night on quiet streets it feels like there are still people. There's noise when you should be feeling silence. This happens to people too. Our deeper strive for peace is the reason you prefer someone who hasn't slept with anyone or many people. We have the awareness in our consciousness that people become too contaminated with energies and become too difficult to rest upon the more they collect other peoples vibrations. Nature is magnetic.

If you raise your consciousness higher, you can tell a person or a place that ◇ been touched by people without having to see s picture or explanations. Not every feeling of hunger means you need to eat. Around midnight if you are awake, you'll notice you suddenly get the urge to eat even if you had a late supper. This doesn't always happen because you had less food for supper but in the midnight hours your mind becomes open to seek further thought. You sink into your mind and generate ideas to solve your problems or make life improvements. The feeling of hunger is in association with mental hunger and you will realize it it temporary if you sit a few minutes without getting up to eat. Feed the consciousness within. Not the stomach. It's part of your story line, not your destination. Stop claiming experiences of bad luck as a bad life. When a tree grows, some leaves fall off, but that's necessary so that the soil can be more fertile for the roots to grow. Bad experiences in your life are a preparation for you to have a better reaction in the future when they happen again. Life is not on a mission to put you down. Be focused.

One day you are going to have to wake up and tell yourself that the suffering is enough. Taking the first step is the hardest but yet the most important. Scars only exist after you heal, not while you bleeding. Before you can declare yourself as cursed, poor or broken, remember that a human doesn't have any nature. They only exist with what they choose to be. Choose to stop the bleeding and the healing process will be your new path. Change doesn't come from opening wounds constantly with bitter words you tell yourself, it comes from taking action different from your source of pain. You were not born to dwell on what makes you suffer while others continue to live comfortably at your expense.

"Nobody is coming to save you from poverty, your life is 100% your responsibility"
– Obakeng Mosime

Chapter 9

BE IN CONTROL OF YOUR LIFE

We often hear the phrase life is a journey but it is not just any journey. It is one that we navigate every single day, making decisions, taking actions, and dealing with the consequences of those choices. This journey is unique in that it is not guided by maps, directions, or any kind of manual. Rather, it is a journey that we must chart ourselves, using our intuition, experience, and wisdom to make our way through. One thing that is common among all people, regardless of age, gender, or ethnicity, is the desire to be in control of their lives.

We all want to feel like we are the ones calling the shots, making the decisions that shape or futures. Unfortunately, this desire often falls short in the face of external factors that seem to dictate our lives. It is easy to feel like we are being pushed and pulled by circumstances beyond our control, leaving us feeling powerless and frustrated. The truth, however, is that we are always in control of our lives, even when it may not seem like it. We may not be able able to control external events, but we can control how we respond to them.

We can choose to react with fear and negativity, or we can choose to approach challenges with optimism and a can-do attitude. The first step to taking control of your life is to be aware of your thoughts and beliefs. Many of us have deep-seated beliefs that limit our potential, such as the belief that we are not good enough, or that success is only reserved for a select few. These beliefs may have been instilled in us at a young age, but they do not have to dictate our present or future. By acknowledging and challenging these limiting beliefs, we can free ourselves from their grip and start to see the world in a new light. Another key element in taking control of your life is to be intentional in your actions. Too often, we allow ourselves to drift through life without a clear sense of direction or purpose.

We may have vague ideas of what we want to achieve, nut we do not take the necessary steps to make those goals a reality. To be intentional means to set clear goals, create a plan to achieve them, and take consistent action towards their attainment. This may require some sacrifice and hard work, but the rewards are well worth it. Taking control of your life also means being responsible for your own happiness. It is easy to fall into the trap of seeking validation and happiness from external sources, such as material possessions, relationships, or social status. While these things may provide temporary satisfaction, true happiness come from within. By cultivating a sense of gratitude, practicing self-care, and surrounding ourselves with positive influences, we can create a foundation of happiness that is not dependent on external factors.

One of the most important aspects of taking control of your life is being adaptable. Life is unpredictable, and there will be times when things do not go according to plan. When this happens, it is important to be able to pivot and adjust our course. This requires a mindset of flexibility and openness to new possibilities. Instead of seeing obstacles as roadblocks, we can view them as opportunities for growth and learning. Ultimately, being in control of your life means taking ownership of your choices and taking responsibility for their outcomes.

It means recognizing that you have the power to shape your own destiny, and that every decision you make has the potential to impact your life in a meaningful way. Write a list of all the people that are avoiding your calls right now. People that you ask to plug you with opportunities and they ghost you. People that close their window when they see you. Write their names. Remember their faces. Remember the relatives that pretend to love you you while your parents were still alive. Relatives that have been ghosting you and your siblings since the funeral. Remember all these people. When you rise, when God lifts you up, keep the same energy. All the hate and disrespect you are getting because you have nothing. Use that as motivation. People are quick to forget.

Make sure you don't forget and only eat with those you were hungry with. Without a stable and focused mind, money will always be unstable in your life. You won't know if it's coming or going. It requires you to be well balanced mentally for you to send it to work for you. Money doesn't stay long where it's not valued. The wealthy want hide and therefore create as many structures, systems and schemes to stay behind the curtains. They want to remain anonymous to the general public, the tax man and other foes in their space.

The new rich always want to be seen and heard, they want to show up and off sticking out like a sore thumb. That's why you will find most of the Forex traders in their 20's drive cars that are too colorful, loud and fast. It attracts a lot of attention and if you can't manage it, it can be detrimental. The most popular ones of the lot were in some way or form almost robbed or killed. The new rich black folk can't move in silence when they make money, that's why they always end up getting in trouble, Paper money is silent, coins make a lot of noise. Let those with ears hear. If you can make your own money with little to no interference from the ills of this country, by all means, do it, and while at that, go off grid ◆ rid yourself of the need to try and save society or the country. You won't. Throughout history, many have tried all over the world to their own detriment. You'll develop heart diseases and disrupt your own life trying to save a nation on autopilot, living for the next bottle of wine, the next trend, the next big song, the next trolling activity.

The only thing you can do is vote better in the hope of change and leave everything else to those who brought us where we are. The ills keep mounting day-after-day. Until the whole nation is ready to speak in one voice, just do you.

Here's important finance and investing basics that every household MUST learn, understand and practice.

Emergency Account: You should save at least 6 to 12 months expenses and hold it in a savings account for any emergencies.

Debts:There's two types of debts: bad debts and good debts. Prioritize paying off all your bad debts, especially those with high interest. Getting yourself out of the rabbit hole must be your priority. Decide a method to use when paying your debts and stick to it until all your bad debts are fully paid off. You can decide between: Avalanche and Snowball. Whatever works for you. Avalanche is paying off minimum payments on all your debts first. Then use any remaining amount to pay extra on the debt with the biggest interest. Snowball is paying all the smallest debts first. Then roll that money you were paying on those small debts to bigger ones. You decide what works for you best. Avoid falling into the debt trap and getting stuck there. You will lose your sleep and die young. Learn about good debts and how to leverage your income to speed up your wealth.

Budgeting: A budget is telling your money where to go, instead of wondering where it went. Build yourself a monthly budget so you know where every rand is going and why. Become intentional with your spending. Inflation: Understand that saving money means losing purchasing power. You cannot save your way to wealth, you must invest. Build your savings pocket to a certain lump sum and then use that lump sum to invest in cash-flow positive generating assets. Rinse and repeat.

How stock market works: Open an EasyEquities account, Invest monthly, learn about shares, ETF's, learn about compound interest and why it helps long term investors win. Short-term fear and volatility doesn't matter to those investing with decades in mind.

Dividends ;The easiest form of passive income that all of us can obtain are dividends. Invest in companies that pays dividends, reinvest your dividends to grow your investment portfolio.

How the banks take advantage of you:

Learn how the banks works, how they make money. Your deposited money in the bank is constantly being loaned out or invested to make the bank money while they give you just a small percentage in return and keep all the profits made. Remember, only save to invest.

Property Investing: Property ownership never go out of style. And when investing in property for rental purposes. That monthly cash flow becomes so valuable. Learn about property investing and go build your empire.

The history of money: Understand our financial system and how it works will help you to see that investing is essential. Assets are the only path to financial freedom and wealth.

Only eat with the ones you starved with
– Obakeng Mosime

Chapter 10

OVERCOMING THE BURDEN OF BLACK TAX

Growing up in a black family comes with many unique challenges, one of which is the burden of black tax. Black tax is the financial obligation that many black individuals face when they reach a certain level of success. It is the unwritten rule that you must support your extended family, regardless of your own financial situation. This burden can be overwhelming and can hinder the financial growth of black individuals. The history of black tax can be traced back to apartheid South Africa, where black individuals were denied opportunities for education and employment.

Many black individuals were forced to leave their families behind in rural areas in search for work. The few black individuals who were able to secure employment often sent money back home to support their families. This financial obligation became known as black tax. Today, black tax has evolved and is no longer limited to South Africa. Many black individuals in different parts of the world face the same burden. As a black individual, I understand firsthand the pressure and responsibility that comes with supporting your extended family. The burden of black tax can be overwhelming for many black individuals, especially those who are just starting their careers or are struggling to make ends meet. Black individuals often feel a sense of obligation to support their families, even if it means sacrificing their own financial well-being. This financial obligation can have a significant impact on their mental and emotional health.

Black tax can also hinder the financial growth of black individuals. Many black individuals are forced to delay their dreams of home-ownership, travel, and retirement because they are supporting their families. This delay can put black individuals at a disadvantage compared to their peers who do not have to support their families financially. While black tax can provide financial support to extended families, it can also create dependency and hinder their financial growth. Some families rely solely on the financial support of one individual, which can create a cycle of dependency that is difficult to break. This cycle can also cause tension and conflict within families.

Black tax can also impact the education of younger family members. Some black individuals are forced to sacrifice their own education to support their families financially. This sacrifice can limit the opportunities available to younger family members who may be relying on their older relatives for financial support. Breaking the cycle of black tax requires a change in mindset and a commitment to financial literacy.

Black individuals must recognize the importance of their own financial well-being and the impact that black tax can have on their future. This requires an understanding of financial literacy and the ability to make informed decisions. Black individuals must also communicate with their families and set boundaries. This can be a difficult conversation to have, but it is necessary to ensure that black individuals are not being taken advantage of financially.

Setting boundaries can also help to break the cycle of dependency and encourage family members to become financially independent. Black individuals must prioritize their own financial goals. This means setting aside money for their own financial well-being, such as retirement, home-ownership, and travel. Prioritizing their own financial goals can help black individuals achieve financial stability and break the cycle of black tax.

"Prioritize your own financial goals and set boundaries"
– Obakeng Mosime

Chapter 11

THE FALLACY OF THE LOTTERY TICKET MENTALITY

We've all heard the saying "you're not a lottery ticket" before. It's a phrase often used to remind people that they can't rely on the idea of getting rich quick to solve their financial problems. However, this mentality extends beyond buying lottery tickets. In fact, it's a pervasive mindset that can have a significant impact on our financial well-being, especially when it comes to giving money to others.

Many people fall into the trap of believing that giving money to others is a way to increase their own wealth. They believe that if they help others, they will be rewarded in some way whether it be through financial gain, karma, or simply feeling good about themselves. However, this mentality is flawed and can actually lead to financial ruin.

The Danger of Giving Money to Others; Giving money to others can be a noble and selfless act. However, when it becomes a habit, it can quickly become dangerous. The problem with giving money to others is that it's often done without any real thought or planning. People give money to others on a whim, without considering the impact it will have on their own finances. This lack of planning can lead to financial strain, especially for those who are already struggling to make ends meet. Giving money to others can deplete your own financial resources, leaving you in worse financial position than before.

This is especially true if the people you are giving money to are not using it responsibly. The fallacy of the lottery ticket mentality is the idea that can rely on luck or chance to solve your financial problems. This mentality can manifest in many ways, from buying lottery tickets to giving money to others. The problem with this mentality is that it takes the focus off of taking responsibility for your own financial well-being.

When we believe that luck or chance will solve our financial problems, we become passive in our approach to finances. We stop taking the necessary steps to improve our financial situation, such as budgeting, saving, and investing. Instead, we rely on external factors to solve our problems, which is a recipe for financial disaster. Breaking the cycle of the lottery ticket mentality requires a shift in mindset. Instead of relying on luck and chance, we need to take an active role in our finances. This means setting financial goals, creating a budget, and making informed financial decisions.

When you are broke nobody respects you. Like it or not money goes hand in hand with respect. Nobody really cares about your opinion. You will not receive phone calls, you won't be told about family meetings because you're not contributing anything. Nobody will borrow you money to fund your goals. Everybody will distance themselves from you. You will struggle alone. The sad part is that people are too quick to forget. The moment you start being financially stable, you will start getting phone calls from people that never called you before. Family members will start calling you telling you about family meetings. Your uncles will start calling you to assist them with finance to solve their sudden recurring financial problems. You will get messages from long lost 'friends' asking for your assistance.

People will start asking for your advice and your opinion will suddenly matter; Funny world we live in isn't it...No matter how dumb your opinion is, people will listen because you now have the power of money backing you. People will respect you, don't let this go to your head and start being an arrogant bum. Focus! All those people disappeared when you were broke. None of them were prepared to lend a helping hand when you needed one. Your rich aunt blue-ticked your messages but now she needs money to fix her car with a sudden amnesia needs your help. This is what I mean by saying people are too quick to forget. Your friend needs money from you to buy electricity.

Everybody wants something from you. Some even feel entitled to your money; people are weird. My advice is Ditch those people they are leeches, they will suck you dry and leave you hanging. When you have money make sure you only eat with those you starved with. Do not give a piece of yourself to anyone who don't deserve it. Reserve your energy, protect your peace. Giving money to those people will only deplete the money that was supposed to be building your wealth and creating a legacy. Take my advice or don't...the choice is yours.

"Giving money to others can deplete your own financial resources, leaving you in worse financial position than before."
– Obakeng Mosime

Chapter 12

LEECHES

Leeches are blood-sucking worms that belong to the phylum annelida and class hirudinea. They are known for their ability to attach themselves to the skin of animals, including humans, and feed on their blood. Leeches are associated with parasitism and being opportunistic creatures that latch onto hosts to obtain nourishment. In this chapter I use the term leech metaphorically to describe people who cling onto others for personal gain, draining resources and energy without giving anything in return.

The uncomfortable truth that is often left unspoken is that many individuals eagerly anticipate the passing of their parents. They are fixated on obtaining the material possessions that will be left behind, such as the family home, car, shop or even the monetary inheritance. Sadly, for a significant number of people, their sole plan for their future revolves around this expected windfall.

They are merely waiting to claim what is not rightfully theirs, hoping to start a new life on someone else's hard-earned assets. Meanwhile, there are others who are actively engaged in making their own plans, working tirelessly to secure their own futures. These individuals understand that they must create their own path in life and not rely on the inheritance of others. However, there are those who remain idle, waiting for the inheritance or insurance money to arrive so they can recklessly spend it all in one go. This is a truly unfortunate reality that highlights the pitfalls of a mentality that is fixated on instant gratification, rather than taking the time to build a life of one's own.

The something called a Moocher. What is that? What does it mean?

A moocher is an individual who constantly seeks to receive things without putting in any effort or contributing anything in return. They have a mindset that the world owes them and feels entitled to receive free clothes, shoes, money, or food.

These individuals can be found among our friends and relatives, always taking but never giving, and lacking any interest in personal growth or seizing opportunities. Their sole purpose is requesting favors, food, or money, displaying a consistent pattern of taking without reciprocating. Moochers lack the understanding of the principle of mutual benefit and instead aim to be the sole beneficiaries. It's important to strive to avoid adopting the mindset of a moocher as it is considered distasteful.

Becareful of Pocket watchers. One may wonder and ask what does that mean. A pocket watcher is always watching your pockets. Someone who always wants to know exactly how much you have. Someone who feels the urge to know how deep are your pockets. Be careful of these kind of people.

You can filter out these people very easy by just observing. When you make a purchase they always want to see the price tag, always want to know the exact amount, they want to know how much money you have. These kinds of people are always watching your pockets and this will lead to jealousy and result in them trying to block your success by any means possible. Some will even go to consult traditional doctors to find out where you getting the money from, and ultimately they will result in them bewitching you to slow down your progress. Anyone who doesn't believe in this, it's perfectly fine, those who know what I'm talking about will relate.

"Whatever you become in life, do not be a moocher."
– Obakeng Mosime

Chapter 13

THE POWER OF THE COMPOUND EFFECT

The power of the compound effect is an undeniable force that can lead to the accumulation of wealth over time. When harnessed correctly, it has the potential to transform the financial fortunes of individuals and families alike. Let us explore how the compound effect works and how it can be used to generate wealth over the long term.

At its core, the compound effect is a simple concept that involves the accumulation of small, incremental gains over time. When these gains are allowed to compound upon themselves, the end result can be a significant increase in wealth. For example, if you invest R1000 and earn 10% return in the first year, you will have R1210. Over time, the gains continue to accumulate, and the final result can be truly remarkable. However, the compound effect is not just about financial gains.

It can also be applied to other areas of life, such as health and relationships. For example, if you make small incremental improvements to your diet and exercise routine, you will gradually become healthier over time. Similarly, if you make small positive changes to your relationship with others, your connections will deepen and strengthen over time. But let's focus on the financial aspect of the compound effect. One of the key principles of the compound effect is that it requires time to work it's magic.

The longer you allow your gains to compound, the greater the end result will be. This is why it's important to start investing early and stay invested over the long term. Another important principle of the compound effect is that it requires consistency. You cannot expect to generate significant wealth through sporadic, one-time investments. Instead, you need to consistently invest over time, regardless of short-term market fluctuations or economic conditions. In addition to consistency, the compound effect also requires discipline. You need to be disciplined enough to resist the temptation to spend your money on frivolous purchases or to try to time the market. Instead, you need to develop a long-term investment strategy and stick to it, even when the going gets tough. Perhaps one of the most powerful aspects of the compound effect is its ability to multiply your gains over time. As your investments grow, they generate their own gains, which then compound upon themselves. This creates a snowball effect that can lead to significant wealth over the long term. For example you invest R10 000 and earn an average annual return of 8%, your investment will grow to over R46 000 after 20 years. If you continue to reinvest your gains, your investment will grow to over R100 000 after 30 years. But the power of the compound effect is not just limited to long-term investments.

It can also be applied to short-term saving goals, such as building an emergency fund or saving for a down payment on a house. By consistently setting aside small amounts of money over time, you can build up a significant amount of savings that can be used to achieve your goals. Of course the compound effect is not the holy grail or a guaranteed path to wealth. It requires discipline, consistency, and patience, and there are no shortcuts or quick fixes. But for those who are willing to put in the work and stay committed over the long term, the rewards can be truly life-changing.

Let us dive deep on this as I put this in a form of a short story about Lebogang's life. Brace yourself.

Lebogang had grown up on the dusty streets of South Africa. His family had struggled to make ends meet, and he had known from a young age that he needed to find a way to rise above his circumstances. But it wasn't until he stumbled upon the power of the compound effect that he truly began to see a way out.

It all started with a small investment. Lebogang had saved up a few hundred rand from odd jobs and decided to invest in a local stock. He didn't expect much from the investment, but he was pleasantly surprised when the stock began to climb in value. It wasn't a huge gain, but it was enough to give him hope. Lebogang started to read more about investing and the power of the compound effect. He learned that by investing small amounts consistently over time, he could generate significant wealth. He began to set aside a portion of his earnings each week and invested it in a variety of stocks and mutual funds. At first, progress was slow.

Lebogang's investment didn't generate huge gains overnight, but he remained committed. He continued to invest consistently, even during times of market volatility or economic uncertainty. He knew that the compound effect would work its magic over time if he remained patient and disciplined. And gradually, it did. Lebogang's investments began to generate larger and larger gains as the years went by. He was able to reinvest his earnings and let the power of the compound effect work its magic. Soon, he was able to use his earnings to support himself and his family, and he was no longer living paycheck to paycheck. But Lebogang wasn't content to simply accumulate wealth for himself. He wanted to use his knowledge and experience to help others rise above their circumstances as well. He began to offer financial advice to his friends and family, and soon he was being approached by strangers on the street who heard about his success.

Lebogang decided to start a financial education program for young people in his community. He wanted to teach them the power of the compound effect and help them take control of their financial futures. The program was a huge success, and soon Lebogang was invited to speak at events and conferences throughout the country. As Lebogang's reputation grew, he began to attract the attention of wealthy investors and entrepreneurs.

They were impressed by his knowledge and his passion, and the saw the potential for a powerful partnership. Soon, Lebogang was working with some of the wealthiest individuals in the country, advising them on their investments and helping them to navigate the complex landscape. Despite his success, Lebogang never forgot where he came from. He continued to live modestly and to support his family and community.

He knew that the power of the compound effect was not just about accumulating wealth, but about using that wealth to make a difference in the world. Years later, Lebogang was approached by a young man who had attended his financial education program many years before. The young man had gone on to start his own successful business and was now a wealthy entrepreneur in his own right. He thanked Lebogang for his guidance and inspiration. And told him that he had changed his life.

Lebogang smiled and shook the young man's hand. He knew that the power of the compound effect was not just about generating wealth, but about changing lives. And he was grateful for the opportunity to make a difference in the world, one investment at a time. It takes a lot of work and a lot of time to become wealthy. Its about thinking in decades but spacing out your targets in 5 year terms for your investment portfolio or business. Interest. Hence Einstein said compound interest is the 8th wonder of the world, if you don't let time work for you, it will work against you nonetheless and the consequences of that are dire.

"Those who are willing to put in the work and stay committed over the long term, the rewards can be truly life-changing."
– Obakeng Mosime

Chapter 14

NO EXCUSES

I want you to understand what I mean by 'No Excuses', so I'm gonna emphasize this through a short story also, this is Karabo's story.

Karabo was a man who always had an excuse for everything in his life. Whenever someone asked him why he hadn't achieved much, he would always blame it on someone else or something beyond his control. "it's not my fault", he would say, "the economy is bad", or "i didn't have the right opportunity." Unfortunately, his excuses had become a habit, and it had resulted in him living a life of poverty and unfulfilled dreams. Karabo had always wanted to start his own business, but he never took the necessary steps to make it happen.

He would often complain that he didn't have the money or the resources to start a business. However, the truth was that he was afraid of failure. He didn't want to take any risks, and he used his excuses as a way to justify his inaction. One day, Karabo met an old friend from high school, Lesego, who had become very successful in the business world. Lesego had started his own company from scratch, and it had grown into a multi million-dollar enterprise. Karabo was envious of Lesego's success, but he also felt a glimmer of hope. If Lesego could do it, maybe he could too. Lesego saw potential in Karabo and offered to mentor him in starting his own business.

Karabo was excited about the opportunity but quickly became overwhelmed with the amount of work required. He would often say "I don't have time" or "I'm too busy with other things." Lesego tried to help Karabo overcome his excuses, but it was a difficult task. Karabo would always find a reason not to take action. Lesego eventually gave up on him and told him, "If you want to be successful, you need to take responsibility for your life and stop making excuses." Karabo was initially upset with Lesego's advice, but deep down, he knew that Lesego was right. He decided to take a hard look at his life and take ownership of his actions. He realized that he had been using his excuses as a crutch and that he needed to break free that mindset. Karabo started small by setting achievable goals for himself. He started reading books on entrepreneurship and attending seminars to learn from successful entrepreneurs. He also started networking with people in his industry to gain insight and knowledge. Over time, Karabo's efforts started to pay off. He secured a small loan and launched his own company, a catering company.

The business started slowly, but with hard work and determination, it started to gain traction. Karabo's catering company began to attract more clients, and he was soon able to expand his offerings. He started to cater for large events and corporate functions. His business began to grow, and he was able to hire employees to help with workload. As Karabo's business grew, so did his confidence. He realized that he had been limiting himself with his excuses and that he had the potential to achieve more than he ever imagined. He started to dream big and set ambitious goals for himself and his business.

Karabo's success did not come without challenges. There were times when he encountered setbacks, and he was tempted to fall back into his old habits of making excuses. However, he had learned from his past mistakes and refused to let his excuses hold him back. Today, Karabo is a successful entrepreneur, and his catering company has become one of the most sought-after in his city. He often speaks at seminars and regarded as a role model for aspiring entrepreneurs.

Karabo's story serves as a lesson that excuses will always hold you back in life. It takes courage and determination to break free from the cycle of excuses and take ownership of your life. With hard work and dedication, you can achieve anything you set your mind to, but you must first take responsibility for your actions and stop making excuses. If you find that your skill is not bringing in money, it may indicate that you are targeting the wrong audience. Alternatively, it could mean that you have not yet mastered the skill. To make money with your skills, it is crucial to achieve mastery by working tirelessly on them every day through practice and repetition.

Investing in your skills and skill sets is essential, and if you observe someone excelling in their skills, remember that it takes a lot of effort and time to get to that level. Even simple tasks like selling on the corner requires overcoming numerous mental barriers. Therefore, focus on mastering your skills and persevere until you see results. Remember that you can always change your life by investing in yourself and your abilities. If you can purchase an item and resell it at a higher price, you have done yourself a great service. However, some individuals were never taught to appreciate the value of even the smallest profits they make from any business venture. Profit is profit, regardless of the amount.

If you buy something for R5 and sell it for R10, that indicates significant progress and can propel you further in funding your business. Although this profit may not fund your lifestyle, it can undoubtedly contribute to your long-term business goals. Unfortunately, we come from a society that often underestimates the value of small profits. This mentality has cost us many industries, to other race, instead of expecting to make millions of profits within a few weeks, we should be patient and understand that success take time. Remember, becoming a millionaire does not happen overnight, but rather it takes consistent effort and time to achieve this. Even if you're financially struggling but have a rich mindset, you can turn things around if you're dedicated, consistent, and committed to your work and skills.

Your breakthrough is just around the corner, so don't lose hope and keep pushing through challenges. Allow yourself time to learn new skills and generate income, and once you do, focus on managing your money wisely. Every setback is an opportunity to learn, grow, and improve, so keep striving for success. Remember, it takes 10 sets of R1000 to earn your first R100k, and 10 sets of 100k to make your first million. Ignore the naysayers and stay focused on your goals to achieve success in your toil. When launching a new business, it may be tempting to undercut your competition by charging lower prices. However, this strategy is unlikely to succeed in the long run. Consumers are drawn to expensive products, even those who may not have much wealth themselves. Poor individuals often choose to spend their money on high-end goods, rather than supporting local, low-cost brands.

This is because the poor tend to perceive successful, wealthy individuals as more worthy of their support. The mentality of a poor person is not to solve the poverty of another poor individual, but to support the rich because it creates an illusion of wealth and status. When setting prices for your products or services, it is important to establish a fair value and stick to it.

The right customers will appreciate and support your business at fair price point. Do not be afraid to charge a premium for quality products, as many consumers prefer luxury items over lower-priced alternatives. While wealthy individuals may seek to pay less, those with less financial means often trust and prefer product that are expensive. Do not go to anyone to complain about not having money to start a business.

Focus on acquiring a rare skill and use that skill to raise money and start small. It doesn't even have to be a rare skill. People are lazy, just find something that will make their lives easier and sell it to them. The reason why so many people don't start is because they're waiting for someone to save them to reach their goals. The goals are yours, raise money for yourself. Let that funding find you half way. People don't believe in ideas, especially if you are still starting. This is why you shouldn't tell people your ideas before you implement them. The internet is full of free useful information so much that nowadays being ignorant and broke is a choice. There are many things you can put into great use. You just have to find the right information, follow the right people and use correct strategies to implement your ideas. Making 50 rand a day from your businesses is a lot. We are living in hard economic times. Any money could make a difference because it's the money you never had.

Ah, the struggles of being a tech-savvy youngster in a world full of clueless parents! It's like we speak a whole different language – they're still stuck on "WhatsApp" while we're living our best lives on smartphones that can do practically anything (except maybe make breakfast, but hey, we're working on it). But let's be real, fellow youngsters, we can't just sit around and make fun of our parents for not understanding AI (Artificial Intelligence) or the tech trends. Sure, they may come to guidance, but until then, it's up to us to take advantage of all the opportunities that these magical devices offer. And yet, some of us still think that making money through our phones is a scam while we willingly donate our hard-earned cash on the online betting sites, Specifically on Betway.

Come on, people! We need to open our minds and explore all the possibilities out there. Who knows, we might even become our own bosses and never have to take orders again (cue to cheers). So, to all my fellow young'uns out there, let's get educated and take advantage of the free Wi-Fi we use for TikTok and other activities (ahem, I won't judge). Answer surveys, sell products, be a middle man – the possibilities are endless. And who knows, maybe one day we'll even teach our parents a thing or two. In light of this, it is incumbent upon parents to impart the importance of hard work to their desired business ventures, they must not only understand financial intelligence and economics but also comprehend the various laws and factors that shape pricing and living standards.

Ultimately, it is essential to instill a sense of respect for these principles and ideas in the younger generation, who seem content to indulge in a languid existence and realistic aspirations that do not align with their daily efforts. Procrastination is the thief of time.

Timidity will get you no where. Laziness will destroy you. I can't tell you how many times I've heard people saying "I will open a business soon." However, I haven't witnessed their businesses. But what's delaying you? Tell you what. People fail in this field because of dependency. 'Oh I'm waiting for my boyfriend to give me money to kickstart' she says. People fail because they want to sell somethings unique to avoid competition or the trend, little did you know that trend is money, competition is money. People fail in this field because of the thought of money.

Laziness is the biggest evils of all time. Money has never been a problem to the big players who have mastered the game. Why want to start a 'buy and sell' business if you know you don't have money to stock? Good deliberate challenge there to justify your laziness. Money will never be a problem if you are smart enough. I can sell you anything without even touching it. That's how the big players operate. Weaponize intelligence. Know how to use other people's money. Don't stock before you find buyers. Saying you need money to start is just another excuse you pulled out from your bag of excuses.

"Focus on mastering your skills and persevere until you see results."
– Obakeng Mosime

Chapter 15

THE POWER OF REPETITION

People generally find doing the same thing repeatedly without a loss of momentum challenging, especially for their own interest and benefit. Yet, they don't seem to mind doing it in someone else's interest, this is why people can work in the same job until retirement, do the same thing everyday, but can't seem to do the same for their own benefit. There's power beyond comprehension in repetition. On the surface, it may seem like doing the same task repeatedly, but beyond that, it creates neural pathways – thought processes that will last a lifetime – it's conditioning and a complete rewiring of the mind. Repetition is reinforcement. Additionally, it has a spiritual element to it that unlocks divine favor.

People do the same thing repeatedly, with the same intent, find success eventually because at a spiritual level, repetition carries a strong message of capacity and unrelenting willpower. One guy I met years ago once told me "There are pockets of knowledge which once you tap into, you evoke the spirit that rules over that area of interest, and by doing so, you become the chosen one to carry forward that respective work you've chosen." From consistency, you receive an ongoing supply of resources, wisdom, knowledge, and divine favor that enable you to continue in your journey, and eventually, you become the master of your craft. The only key is consistency.

Repetition in its nature creates and reinforces a process – a process delivers results. For instance, for over 300 weeks I have consistently updated the data to the framework I use to analyze the financial markets, without fail, because of its importance, and I continue doing so every single week. As a result, I have become totally dependent on the framework, and would never dare to attempt analysis on any currency or equity without a glimpse of the relevant data. This is what systems and processes are designed for, to serve as a success-blueprint and keep us from doing that which we shouldn't, in the prevention of yielding undesired results.

However, it all starts with doing one thing repeatedly over an extended period of time, until it becomes engraved in our minds and becomes systematic. Taking small steps towards improvement each day, even if it's just 1% can be more feasible and satisfying. It helps to establish positive habits and gradual progress can lead to significant outcomes over time. Instead of overwhelming yourself with major changes, concentrate on moving in the right direction and making steady advancements. This approach increases the likelihood of achieving success in your pursuits. Furthermore, focusing on making small improvements each day can help us establish positive habits. When we commit to doing something small each day, it becomes easier to make that a routine part of our lives.

These routines can help us build discipline and consistency, which are essential for achieving our long-term goals. Whether it's reading for 10 minutes before bed, writing a journal each morning, or going for a short walk after dinner, these small habits can have a powerful impact on our lives. Making 1% improvement each day can also help us to stay motivated. When we set lofty goals for ourselves, it can be challenging to stay motivated when we don't see immediate progress. By focusing on making small, incremental improvements, we can celebrate our successes more frequently, which can help keep us motivated and energized. Another advantage of this approach is that it helps us to avoid procrastination.

When we set massive goals for ourselves, it's easy to put them off until later. However, when we focus on making small improvements each day, we remove the pressure of having to accomplish everything at once. This makes it easier to get started and can help us avoid the temptation to procrastinate. Furthermore, making 1% improvements each day can help is to build momentum. When we make progress towards our goals, it becomes easier to continue making progress. This can create a snowball effect, where our small improvements compound into significant results over time. Before we know it, we've accomplished more than we thought possible, all because we started with small, achievable goals.

"There's power beyond comprehension in repetition"
– Obakeng Mosime

Chapter 16

SMART MONEY

Money should be kept in one's possession for as long as possible, as it has a tendency to attract and multiply itself. By holding onto money, I am allowing it to work for me and increase my wealth. It's a similar concept to how your employer holds onto your salary until payday – they understand the importance of having money in their account and not giving it away too quickly. Money is an essential part of our lives. It is the medium of exchange that we use to buy goods and services that we need and want. However, the way we handle money can differ greatly, and it's important to understand the concept of smart money.

Smart money refers to the idea of making wise financial decisions and taking control of your finances. It involves making informed decisions about spending, saving, and investing. Smart money management is not just about having more money. It's about knowing how to use your money to achieve your financial goals. For many people, the concept of smart money is not new. They have been practicing smart money management for years, and as a result, they have been able to achieve financial success. However, for some, it is a new concept, and they may not know where to start.

Smart money is important for several reasons. Firstly, it helps you to achieve financial stability. When you make informed decisions about spending and saving, you are less likely to find yourself in a situation where you are struggling to make ends meet. Smart money management can help you to create a financial safety net, which can give you peace of mind. Secondly, smart money management can help you to achieve your financial goals. Whether you want to buy a house, save for retirement, or start a business, smart money management can help you to get there faster.

When you are in control of your finances, you make strategic decisions that will help you to achieve your goals. Finally, smart money management can help you to build wealth. When you invest your money wisely, you can grow your wealth over time. Smart money management can help you to make the most of your money and create a better financial future for yourself and your family. There are several key principles of smart money management. These principles can help you to make informed decisions about your finances and achieve your financial goals.

Budgeting; The first principle of smart money management is budgeting. A budget is a plan that outlines your income and expenses for a specific period. By creating a budget, you can track your spending and ensure that you are living within your means. To create a budget, start by listing all of your sources of income.

This might include your salary, rental income, or investment income. Next, list all of your expenses, including your fixed expenses. Once you have listed your income and expenses, subtract your expenses from your income to see if you have a surplus or a deficit. If you have a surplus, consider saving or investing the extra money. If you have a deficit, look for ways to reduce your expenses or increase your income. The unfortunate reality is that many people go to bed hungry and struggle to make ends meet. This is often due to the fact that we tend to focus on our immediate needs and wants, rather than planning for the future. For instance, out of a group of 100 people who have a stable income, only a single individual may invest their money to build long-term wealth.

This shortsightedness may lead to difficulties for future generations who rely on the resources we leave behind. To ensure a better future for our descendants, we should prioritize investing our earnings rather than spending them on fleeting luxuries like fancy cars or vacations. As a black man, I am determined to break the cycle of poverty in my family and ensure that future generations are not left to struggle as I did.

Ultimately, we must recognize that we are responsible for our own well-being and the welfare of our descendants, rather than relying on others to provide for us. When someone is living in poverty, owning a house becomes a top priority, and they will struggle tirelessly to achieve that goal. However, when someone has sufficient financial resources, they are less likely to prioritize buying a house. Instead, they focus on investing their wealth to grow it even further.

This stark difference in priorities highlights the significant wealth gap between the rich and the poor. As the rich becomes richer, they are able to focus on their own self-interests, while the poor continue to struggle to make ends meet. The ability to invest in profitable ventures is not available to everyone, and those living in poverty may have few options for increasing their wealth.

This is why owning a home becomes so important for those living in poverty. It represents a tangible asset that they can own and protect, and it provides a sense of security that is often lacking in their lives. If you avoid taking risks and fear failure, and don't have the courage to get up and keep going after failing, you will never achieve success. Building wealth is a common aspiration for many people, and there are various ways to achieve this goal. One of the most effective strategies is to generate income through various means such as running a business, having a job, or pursuing side toils, and then investing that money wisely. This can provide an avenue for growth and expansion of wealth over time.

One way to invest is by purchasing shares in companies through the stock market. By doing so, you can own a piece of a company and potentially earn dividends and capital gains as the company grows. Shares can be bought and sold relatively easily, and it's possible to invest in a variety of companies across different sectors and regions. However, investing in shares comes with some risks, such as fluctuations in the market and company performance, so it's essential to do thorough research before investing.

Investing in property can also be a smart way to build wealth over the long term. Property prices tends to appreciate over time, and rental income can provide a steady source of cash flow. Owning property can also provide a sense of stability and security, as it's a tangible asset and can be passed down through generations. However, investing in property requires a significant amount of capital upfront and comes with ongoing costs such as maintenance and property taxes.

Crypto investments have become increasingly popular in recent years, with the rise of digital currencies such as Bitcoin and Ethereum. Investing in crypto can potentially provide high returns, but it also comes with high volatility and risk. It's important to thoroughly research the market and invest only what you can afford to lose. Rare collections, such as art, antiques, or rare coins, can also be a valuable investment. These items can appreciate in value over time and can be a unique and enjoyable asset to own. However, investing in rare collections requires expertise and knowledge, as it's important to identify genuine items and understand market trends.

Investing in other small businesses can also be a smart way to build wealth over time. By investing in other entrepreneurs, you can potentially earn a share of their profits and support the growth of innovative ideas. However, investing in small businesses comes with risks, as many startups fail within the first few years. It's essential to conduct thorough due diligence and invest only in companies that align with your values and have a strong track record. Regardless of the investment strategy, it's important to maintain a mindset of being financially conservative by acting broke.

This means living below your means and prioritizing savings and investment over frivolous spending. By doing so, you can maximize your potential for growth and expansion of wealth over time. Another thing you should know about money is that it is valuable only as long as it is being used. Once it has been taken out of circulation, it becomes as worthless as the "old newspapers" or "empty beer cans" that have been stashed away in the attic.

Money is not meant to be hoarded. Rather, it is meant to be used, enjoyed and circulated. Please note that when is suggest that money should be kept in circulation, I do not mean it should be squandered. There is a world of difference between those two concepts and if you haven't found out what the difference is yet, I would suggest you find out as soon as possible. Money will have a greater influence on your life than almost any other commodity you can think of.

Money is a servant; you are the master. Be very careful not to reverse that equation. Because many people of high intelligence have already done so, to their great detriment. Unfortunately, many of these poor souls loved money and used people. Which violated one of the most basic laws governing true financial success. You should always love people and use money, rather than the reverse.

Another myth many people like to accept about money is that it only comes as a result of "luck" or "good fortune." for instance, whenever people gather to talk about someone they know who has been financially successful, there is always someone among them who will say, "Obakeng was just lucky," or "Obakeng was just in the right place at the right time." But I want to assure you in no uncertain terms, that although "luck" obviously plays some part in financial success, it is never sufficient in and of itself. Money is an effect and it must always be earned. Believe me, there are no free rides in this life and the only people who are making money easy way either work in the mint or are on their way to jail, if they have not already arrived there. Therefore, always bear in mind that while "good fortune" is a factor in financial success, it must always be coupled with effort and hard work.

Most people still think success is luck or talent. But success is rather discipline, perseverance, and having the hindsight to learn from your failures. The truth is you're going to stumble, fall, and fail a lot. It's inevitable, just keep learning from it. Don't shy away from it embrace it and keep moving forward. Only through this process of trial and error can you achieve greatness. Saving money is good but investing is better. The problem with saving is that if you have 20 thousand today, 5 months later it will still be 20 thousand. Investing is better. When you invest your money grows. Instead of 20 thousand, you now have 40 thousand. 5 months is a long time for money to just sit around. Make your money work, put your money to good use. It's good to save but don't save all your money. Invest in different places, never invest all your money in one place. To become wealthy you need to do what the wealthy people are doing. Wealthy people spend their time looking for business and investment opportunities.

Wealthy people invest in assets. A van, goats, dividends, vintage cars, tractor, and rental properties. Silent partner in a business, acquiring skill, etc...wealthy people spend less and increase their income. A wealthy person sees 200 Rand as a lot of money that can generate income while ordinary people treat 200 Rand like it has no value. Some kids are taught how to sell while others are taught how to buy, then years later we wonder why not a single shop in the villages is owned by someone in the village. After studying the 'Smart Money Elites', I came to an understanding that wealthiest individuals value time and they monitor how they spend their day. The know how the following day is going to play out because they note everything down and follow a strict schedule.

How you spend your time will determine your future. You need to spending more time on the building and growing phase. Instead of planning to go out and have drinks with your friends or colleagues on a weekend, what you should be doing is re-valuating plans, strategizing, planning for the week ahead, learning new skills or improving your current skills.

Weekends are for execution. Putting our plans to action. On assets and liabilities. The layman's understanding of these 2 terms is that an asset is anything that puts money into your pocket and a liability is anything that put money into your pocket. Notice how I repeatedly talk about assets and liabilities throughout the whole book. I did this on purpose to instill this idea into your mind to always think in terms of assets and liabilities before making a purchase.

You can make anything a liabilities or an asset. It all depends on your mindset and knowledge. That's why you find firms like KKR that buy out other firms that are classified as liabilities, on the books of a multi-billion dollar holding company and turn them into cash churning profitable machines, because they have to know how to turn this seemingly dead liability that is too far out of the realms of being brought back to life, as per the report by top turn around consultants.

I once read of how a businessman bought the latest Range Rover after he got a payout, all because he wanted to maintain an image that his company is big and that he was a successful businessman, but in actual fact it was carefully crafted and riskiest gamble to date, he was trying to sell that perception to his possible clients that were coming for a meeting and if they didn't agree on a deal he would go bankrupt because he only had about 6 months worth of payroll left after having bought the vehicle cash. After the meeting was done as he was seeing them off to their vehicles, he made it a point to hand his employee, who was his 'supposed driver' to put in his documents in the back seat. It was but a stunt for them to see he was the owner of the latest Range Rover, and duly impressed they were. After having concluded the deal, many months whilst having a casual conversation one of the leaders of the delegation confided in him privately and said the car you drove was a key deciding factor in me having given your company with so little experience such a huge contract.

We didn't want to give this contract to anyone that needed it to survive and had little years in the business, such as what your company had, but we wanted to deal with an established and reputable operator, and that you were doing something right to afford such posh top of the line vehicle. He used that contract to get other contracts from referrals and proof of work after having worked with such a company and in turn build a strong and growing business. Money flows to money, people invest with winners or those they think can win with proper guidance and structures. Learn to turn perception into reality, but make sure you can deliver when you are given the job.

There is a time in your life that you should only be worried about investing in your personal growth and what you are building. Don't spend money on looking rich in a bid to compete with your age mates, by eating your seeds that should have gone to being reinvested in your next cycle of growth. Its okay to not drive a fancy car, live in a penthouse or being able to eat at a fancy restaurant in your early stages of building. Most entrepreneurs will literally invest every rand or dollar back into their business. Elon Musk invested every penny of his $100m share he got from PayPal into all 3 of his companies, he had no money for rent, and lodged with friends. They understand that if they don't have a solid base they can't scale and reach the very heights they aspire to, even if they could have. Its that important.

You can't pay to skip the process of going through the pain. Its the most important, it builds character, and it is also the time where most fold under pressure. Being broke after investing is not the same as being broke after spending money on fast cars, traveling, and expensive dinners in a bid to signal your being "I've made it" to all the suitors who had rejected you previously and to those who suggested you would not be much in life.

Most will go back to having nothing just to prove to people that they ate, drove, and went where their detractors never have, even if it's for few years, they will still relish on the past moment...Its silly but happens all the time. Keep investing in yourself, craft, or business it may not pay off now but it will eventually pay off in the future. Even if it takes a decade as long as you learn from your mistakes. Iterate and persist, mathematically you will only lose if you quit. Keep showing up, taking aim and shooting eventually even a novice hunter will one day return with game that he will need assistance with to bring home. I don't personally know Elon Musk but I am sure he never thought he would be the 1st person in the world to build and run 3 billion dollar companies at one time, that would make him one of the wealthiest man alive in recent history with a networth at its height of over $300billion at one time, all that from $100million seed. Keep building, leave the naysayers, there is no comment section on Forbes.

"To ensure a better future for our descendants, we should prioritize investing our earnings rather than spending them on fleeting luxuries like fancy cars or vacations."
– Obakeng Mosime

Chapter 17

START NOW : Acquire new skills

There is no denying the fact that the world we live in today is rapidly changing. With advancements in technology and the constant evolution of industries, the skills that were in demand yesterday might not hold the same value tomorrow. The only way to stay relevant and ahead of the game is to continuously acquire new skills. But why is acquiring skills so crucial, and what are the benefits of doing so? In this chapter, we will explore the power of acquiring skills and how it can transform your life.

The Benefits of Acquiring Skills

Acquiring skills can have a multitude of benefits, both personal and professional. Let's take a closer look at some of the advantages of expanding your skill set. Personal growth: Learning new skills can help you grow as an individual. It can expand your knowledge, challenge your beliefs, and increase your confidence. When you acquire a new skill, you become more sell-aware and gain a deeper understanding of your strengths and weaknesses.

Professional Advancement: In today's competitive job market, acquiring new skills is essential to stay relevant and advance in your career. Employers are always on the lookout for individuals with a diverse skill set that can add value to their organization.

– Financial Stability: Acquiring new skills can also lead to financial stability. With an expanded skill set, you become more marketable and can command higher salaries.

– - Improved Quality of Life: When you have a diverse skill set, you open up opportunities to pursue different interests and passions. This can lead to a more fulfilling and enjoyable life.

Acquiring new skills is not only beneficial, but it's also essential to thrive in today's fast-paced world. The power of acquiring skills lies in it's ability to open doors to new opportunities, enhance personal growth, and lead to professional success.

– Opens Doors to New Opportunities: Acquiring new skills opens doors to new opportunities that you might not have considered before. For example, learning a new language can lead to opportunities to work in a different country, or acquiring digital marketing skills can lead to opportunities to work in a fast-growing industry.

– Enhances Personal Growth: Acquiring new skills can enhance personal growth and self-awareness. When you learn new skills, you push yourself outside of your comfort zone, which can lead to personal growth and self-discovery. It can also increase your confidence and self-esteem, which can have a positive impact on all aspects of your life.

– Leads to Professional Success: Acquiring new skills is crucial for professional success. As industries evolve, new skills become necessary, and those who don't acquire them risk becoming obsolete. When you have a diverse skill set, you become more marketable and command higher salaries. It can also lead to career advancement and opportunities for leadership positions. How to Acquire New Skills Acquiring new skills is not something that happens overnight, it requires dedication, hard work, and a commitment to continuous learning. Here are some tips on how to acquire new skills:

– Identify Your Goals: The first step to acquiring new skills is to identify your goals. What do you want to achieve? What skills do you need to achieve your goals? Once you have identified your goals, you can create a plan to acquire the necessary skills.

– Take Classes or Courses: Taking classes or courses is great way to acquire new skills. You can enroll in online courses or attend in-person classes.

Attend Workshops or Conferences: Attending workshops or conferences is another way to acquire new skills. These events offer an opportunity to learn from experts in the field and network with other professionals.

Read Books or Listen to Audiobooks.

Acquiring skills is essential for success in life, and one skill that is particularly valuable is selling. Surprisingly, this skill is not usually taught in school, which highlights its immense worth. Those who do acquire this skill can stand out in the marketplace, as it is a critical factor in one's survival. In my experience, the most important life skills are often learned outside of formal education, such as though seminars, audio programs, books, and networking with successful businesspeople. Basic selling, persuasion, and negotiation abilities are vital for anyone hoping to succeed in business. While academic achievements and credentials are important, it's a person's ability to persuade others that ultimately leads to success and advancement.

Sales are an exceptional opportunity for those seeking to work independently, be accountable for their own success, and achieve their dreams. With just a pen and a drive to excel, one can pursue their goals without limit. To achieve success in sales, it's crucial to commit to continuous learning and mastery of the craft. In doing so, the rewards are abundant.

Sales is a timeless art, and those who master it are always in demand. When you have control over the entire sales cycle, you have freedom to sell any product, go where you want, and know that your dreams are withing reach. The importance of sales cannot be overstated; it drives the entire economy, and without salespeople, production, distribution, and advertising would all come to a halt.

You also need these two skills to survive financially A skill to make a living and a skill to make a fortune. Your living skill will put bread on the table and your fortune skill will make you wealthy. Specialize until you are special. Look for a rare skill, perfect it and use it as leverage to be successful. We are all on the journey of becoming, no one is exempt from reality. Nature abhors vacuum, if you aren't progressing you are by default regressing. Nobody stays the same place, you are either moving up the pecking order or falling behind. Let's break it down, if you have a million in your account and don't touch it for 15 years the effects of inflation will have eroded the purchasing power of it substantially although it remains the same amount on paper.

You don't get to build muscle mass for 10 years and keep it perfectly cut if don't keep on gymming. The law of gravity will cause it to wither and start sagging especially as old age comes. No business maintains an untouchable space in the market, you adapt, innovate or perish on your knife of ego. A billion dollar market leading company that has a "supposed" monopoly in the market and doesn't see the need to morph because they have a superior product offering can be rendered useless by 6 guys in their 20's that have determined to build the next behemoth using new technological advances as leverage to cut into the market. The market is a ruthless place to become complacent, there is always somebody coming after your lunch. Become undeniably great, but remain agile and teachable if you want to entrench your place.

"It's crucial to commit to continuous learning and mastery of the craft. In doing so, the rewards are abundant."
– Obakeng Mosime

Chapter 18

MONETIZE YOUR SKILLS

Those who believe "money can't buy happiness," didn't consider the freedom that comes from no longer needing a job to live the life you want. If study people who are successful, you will come to the realization that only 32% of all billionaires inherited their money. The rest of the billionaires typically came from poor families and went to build unparalleled financial freedom. 80% of all millionaires are also self-made and came from poor families. Your background can either be a roadblock or your motivation to succeed. Its all up to you.

Entrepreneurship is a state of mind. It isn't merely about implementation of an idea. It is risk taking and trying to create something out of nothing. One must start small and focus on execution, work towards measurable offers and take a leadership into that realm. Acquire a skill and monetize it. The money isn't in knowing more. The money is in execution. If knowing more was so profitable, then all scientists or historians would be wealthy.

You can get traction by having enough knowledge and experience and excellent executing skills. Many people overrate the idea. You see people who start a business focusing on some big problem. That can be sensible as people pay for things if you solve their problem. However, it is better to make sure that you focus on executing that idea. Many businesses are making a lot of money starting businesses that really aren't solving any problem. Remember that there are countless multi millionaires who got rich from the trash business.

They weren't focusing on some grand idea. They merely got rich execution in areas where 'nobody' seems to want to compete. The key thing is also being consistent, persistent, taking risks, and persevering. Mike Tyson once said " Everybody has a plan until they get punched in the mouth." You can have boundless energy, an intense, white-hot drive, and dreams so big they wake you up in a sweat every night, but if you don't dominate all areas of your life, you will collapse under the many forms destructive forces take.

Dominating your space starts with you, you must be a leader in all areas. If you can dominate your own thinking, and all the public's thinking, then you own the space. It's not true that it takes money to make money. The truth is that it takes courage to make money; 80 percent of all millionaires today are first-generation millionaires. They didn't inherit their money or start with money. You have to be courageous to connect with new customers, get more attention, and dominate your customers so that they think of no one else.

Making money, keeping money, and then multiplying money requires monster commitment, dedication, and an obsession with growth. If you work for someone else, take responsibility for growing the company, not just earning a paycheck. That will stack the deck for both your employer and you. Don't be a mere spectator when it comes to making money. Be sure you are on the field trying to score. There is so much money on this planet it is mind boggling, yet most people have next to none.

Most people don't have money because they believe there is a shortage of money, or they believe they don't deserve it or that it's hard to get. I take the attitude that money is everywhere. Everyone has money, and if they are treated right and provided with what they asked for (and more than that), they will happily give me their money. My battle cry is "who's got my money? When I was a young salesman at Truworths store and I needed new shoes or a new pair of jeans, I would show up to work and ask myself, who's got my money for my new shoes and a pair of jeans?

I would look for a customer to open and account and buy directly from me that I get incentive for bringing in a customer. You want revenue? Instead of being obsessed with never having enough, focus on how much money there is and on getting in front of those people who need what you're offering. Money is everywhere and my goal is to get mine. Dream big, but start small. And moreover: work smart. Starting small does not mean that you will need ten years to make it.

Your aim should be choosing business models that will start paying you fast. Use the power of social media to your advantage. Focus on building your brand by creating killer content and getting that content some traction by building a community, one email, one comment, one tweet, one status update at a time. Once you feel you've grown to a point where your brand is sticky and your audience has made your content a regular, even necessary, part of their community and their online experience, you can start to actively create revenue. Unlike in the beginning, where you threw a big net into a big pond to capture in as many members of the socials media school of fish as possible, you're now going to drop in your line to a variety of small ponds. Be patient. In time, if you continue to toil, you'll grow your presence and improve your skills to the point where the fish -really, really big fish – will be jumping straight into your hands. Specialize Until You are special. Once you acquire a skill that is needed by people, weaponize that as a special super power you have and generate income. But don't get comfortable because the world is evolving and things change. Information is easily accessible. Somewhere out there, there's someone hungrier than you putting more hours than you, so specialize until you are special. However, never do anything you're good at for free.

"Dream big, but start small."
– Obakeng Mosime

Chapter 19

7 STEPS TO ZERO DEBT: Unlocking financial freedom

Debt can be a heavy burden, causing stress and limiting our financial freedom. However, with careful planning and determination, it is possible to break free from the chains of debt and achieve a life of financial independence. In this chapter we will explore seven actionable steps that can lead you on the path to zero debt. By implementing these strategies, you will gain control over your finances, reduces your debt, and pave the way to brighter and more prosperous future.

Step 1: Assess your debt and create a budget. The first step towards eliminating debt is to gain a clear understanding of your financial situation. Take a comprehensive look at all your debts, including your credit cards, loans, and outstanding bills. Once you have a complete picture, create a realistic budget that aligns your income with your expenses. Identify areas where you can cut back on discretionary spending and allocate those savings towards your debt repayment plan.

Step 2: Prioritize and organize your debts. Not all debts are created equal. Some may carry higher interest rates or have more severe consequences for non-payment. Prioritize your debts based on these factors. Start by paying off high-interest debts first, such as credit card balances, as they tend to accrue more interest over time. Simultaneously, continue making minimum payments on other debts to maintain a good credit history.

Step 3: Negotiate with creditors. Don't be afraid to reach out to your creditors to negotiate better terms. Many creditors are willing to work with you to create a more manageable payment plan or even reduce the total amount owed. Engage in open and honest communication, explaining your situation and demonstrating your commitment to paying off your debts. By renegotiating terms, you can ease the burden and accelerate your journey towards zero debt.

Step 4: Explore debt consolidation. If you find yourself juggling multiple debts with varying interest rates and payment schedules, consider consolidating them into a single loan. Debt consolidation allows you to combine your debts into one manageable payment. Often with lower interest rate. This simplifies your financial obligations and provides a clear path towards becoming debt-free. Step 5: Increase your income whole cutting expenses is crucial, it's equally important to explore opportunities to increase your income. Consider taking up a side job or freelancing gig to supplement your primary source of income. Utilize your skills and hobbies to earn extra money that can be directly allocated towards debt repayment. This additional income significantly accelerate your progress towards zero debt.

Step 6: Adopt a frugal lifestyle. Living frugally is an effective way to reduce expenses and redirect funds towards paying off debt. Evaluate your spending habits and identify areas where you can make meaningful cutbacks. This could involve reducing dining out, canceling unused subscriptions, or finding more cost-effective alternatives for everyday items. By embracing a frugal lifestyle, you'll not only save money but also cultivate healthy financial habits for the long term.

Step 7: Seek professional guidance if you find yourself overwhelmed or unsure of how to navigate your debt repayment journey, seeking professional guidance can be invaluable. Consider consulting with a reputable financial advisor who can assess your situation, provide personalized advice, and help you create a tailored debt management plan. Their expertise can provide clarity and assist you in making informed decisions as you work towards achieving zero debt. Becoming debt-free requires discipline, determination, and a well-executed plan. By following these seven steps, you can take control of your finances, reduce your debt, and ultimately achieve financial freedom.

"A person who asks questions gets clarity."
-Obakeng Mosime

Conclusion

Throughout this book, we have explored the fundamental principles and practices that empower individuals to embrace success as a choice. We have learned that success begins with a clear vision, a deep understanding of our passions, and a burning desire to make a difference in the world. We have discovered that success is not limited to one area of life – be it personal, professional, or spiritual.

Above all, we have come to understand that success is not an isolated achievement but a journey that encompasses growth, learning, and continuous improvement. It is about embracing failure as a stepping stone to success and maintaining the courage to persevere in the face of challenges.

Success is not a destination but a lifelong commitment. It is a choice we make everyday, in every moment, to pursue our dreams, overcome our fears, and live life to its fullest potential.

May the insights, strategies, and inspiring anecdotes shared within these pages serve as a guiding light on your path to success, embrace the power within you, unleash your potential, and let your actions speak volumes about the choices you make.

About the author

Obakeng Mosime is an entrepreneur, author, and a financial market analyst. The founder of Lucrativefx, founder of BrightN'clean detergents and an Equity investor. His first book is Smart Money Footprints based on the financial markets.
Born and bred in Kuruman – Northern Cape (South Africa). Obakeng comes from a family of 4, with 3 younger brothers, he's the first born. He describes his upbringing as being the Alchemist; he always found a way to start something out of nothing, always had an entrepreneur spirit. As a young man from a disadvantaged background of poverty he's on a mission to rise above all obstacles despite facing a lot of challenges. "Giving up is not an option"-Obakeng Mosime

Acknowledgments

I like to take a moment and thank myself. I am proud of myself. I know that sounds odd, but I want to thank me for persevering, for not giving up, for always pushing myself to the limit in order to achieve my goals. I want to thank me for going the extra mile and putting in those extra hours while others were sleeping. I want to give this message to the future me; "No matter how hard it gets, remember why you started. It's about planting a seed that will grow over a period of time."

Motshweneng

Khiba

Ntsime ntsimana

Pati

Mohurutsi

Jola

Jolinkomo

Mphankomo

Ngwanya

Zwelibanzi

Mpondomise